Greenville, South Carolina

What Is Truth?

Coart Ramey, M.A.
Bryan Smith, Ph.D.

Project Editor: Michael Santopietro
Design: John Bjerk and Duane Nichols
Composition: Jennifer Hearing

Photo credits appear on page 156.

ISBN 978-1-57924-842-0

15 14 13 12 11 10 9 8 7 6 5 4 3

CONTENTS

Introduction

Yes, it's a textbook. I know it doesn't look like one, but it is. It's supposed to teach you something if you put some effort into it. Not that this is a normal textbook—but before I go there, allow me to introduce my esteemed colleague and myself.

My name is Coart. (You say it just like *court.*) I wrote the first half of this book. My friend Bryan wrote the second half. Bryan just finished his doctorate after eight years of work, and he's really happy. You can notice the "Ph.D." after his name on the copyright page and take comfort in the fact that you are in a real doctor's care.

Now, about this book. We don't want anyone confused or surprised by what we're doing, so I'm going to spell it all out right here. The subject of this book is worldviews. A person's worldview is the way he perceives reality and thinks about higher, transcendent ideas like the universe, religion, and the purpose of life. Everyone has a worldview; even if you never think about transcendent ideas, the fact that you don't shows your worldview.

The purpose of this book is to show that the Christian worldview is superior to four other popular worldviews—Hinduism, Buddhism, secular humanism, and postmodernism. The goal of this book is to present all five worldviews accurately and fairly, and in so doing demonstrate for you why Christianity is incomparably better. Although we are trying to present each non-Christian worldview as it really is, obviously we are not objective, disinterested investigators: we firmly believe Christianity is right and the rest are wrong. If you want to read material by someone who is objective and disinterested about absolute truth and the eternal destiny of human beings, you'll have to read some other book, if such a one even exists.

As for the procedure of this book, it is probably different from most other textbooks. Though it might seem new and strange, the approach we take is actually *old* and strange. It was quite common during the Enlightenment, when formal education was concerned with logic and philosophy. Our approach is that of fictitious dialogue, in which made-up characters discuss and dispute different sides of an issue. The advantages to this approach are as follows:

1. It's more interesting reading than an average textbook. Characters have emotions, interact, interrupt each other, argue, and so on.

2. It's more like a real setting in which you would encounter different worldviews. You are likely to run into these ideas in college and in your future workplace, as you're sitting and eating and talking with other people in an informal way.

3. It's easier for the mind to organize data and follow the flow of development. You may not agree, since this book seems less organized than a normal textbook, but we think that activating a reader's imagination makes the material less tiring to read and easier to remember.

We are not insulting your intelligence by assuming you'll think these characters are real people. Actually, we assume you would have figured that out even without this introduction. It may be that a real Buddhist or a real humanist would do a better job defending his beliefs than Li or Ted. But our characters do the best that Bryan or I could do if we were defending their points of view.

Sooner or later, you will face the choice of what you will believe. Nothing can prevent that time from coming. Nothing can keep you from being woven into a mesh of humanity; you are part of a group of people who influence you and whom you influence in turn. Being a human was not your choice, but it is a great privilege that you obviously cannot refuse. Even death itself won't end your existence now that it has begun. The privilege of being human brings with it a tremendous responsibility. We want to point you to Someone who can show you how to fulfill your responsibility in a greater and more wonderful way than any of us can imagine.

What matters most to us is that you know and trust the Lord Jesus. The last thing we want is for you to turn against Christ and embrace a different worldview, such as one of those discussed in this book. But we think you must choose Christ out of knowledge, knowledge both of Christianity and of non-Christian religions.

The world you live in is more closely-knit and eclectic than it has been since the Tower of Babel. In a way, that is great; in another way, dangerous. Wherever on earth you live, you will come into contact with more ideas, philosophies, and religions than your parents or grandparents did. This is great because it broadens your knowledge of the human race and because it allows you to influence many other people for good. It is dangerous because you'll encounter more errors (and lies) that have to be evaluated and rejected.

You live in an exciting time. You have more opportunities and advantages than anyone before you, but you must be ready to meet the challenges.

Welcome now to our fictional presentation of two ordinary, unchurched boys, who encounter five very real worldviews. Enjoy it, remember the facts you learn, and above all, think as you read.

"What happened? Where are we?"

"Dunno. Weird."

"Do you think this is it? Could this be enlightenment, or nirvana, or something, and because we were talking about it, it happened?" I was excited, but Brad stayed calm.

"Maybe," he said. "Or maybe somebody's writing a book about it and we got sucked into the book by talking about it all."

"But don't you both want to find the truth?" This question came from a girl's voice, and since no girls had been in my room a minute earlier, she got our immediate attention.

"Who are you?" we asked in chorus. She was our age, but she looked Indian, like an *India* Indian, not an American Indian.

"I am your guide," she replied, smiling. "I'll lead your investigation of things that were, things that are, and things that yet will be." I was trying to make the connection to Ebenezer Scrooge when Brad spoke, suspicion in his voice.

"Sure you are. But just where are you from, and what is your name?" The girl looked uncomfortable, as if trying to remember something. "Hmp!" Brad hmped. "I know what you are. You're a literary creation, a product of some writer's imagination, have no name or home, and exist purely for the sake of some story. Isn't that right?"

The girl looked hurt, but she spoke proudly. "Maybe I am, but I'm a lot more than that! Do you think any character is wholly made up? I come from a rich family of experiences and memories of good, real people. I react like a real person, and I have feelings like a real person!"

"Oh never mind him," I said. "He's always down on people. He's a cynic."

"Oh!" The girl's eyes lit up. "Good! We'll need him, then. But it's time to get going, boys. We haven't got all year."

"So do we get to name you ourselves, then? I like girls named Bertha. How's that sound?" The girl looked hurt again, but Brad was only joking, I think. We debated a few seconds, but since we don't know any Indian names (we're both from Indian*a*) we settled on Guide Girl, or Guide for short.

Things were strange already, and they got stranger from here. Guide Girl took us out of the mysterious green nothingness my room had dissolved into and led us into a big room like a gym. There were round tables everywhere. People sitting around the tables were talking and laughing, some loudly. A few people walked around, either buzzing in on tables or just looking lost.

"Where shall you begin?" Guide Girl wanted to know.

"The snack stand," said Brad. "I'm half starved."

"You can eat at the tables—some of the tables. Really now, we are here to engage in the Conversation. Go on, then, select one."

"They all look pretty full," I observed.

"Oh please, there are always enough chairs. Now do please decide."

I wasn't much liking Guide Girl's hoity attitude, but Brad reminded me that I hadn't eaten since we split a pizza two hours ago, and I was getting hungry myself.

We saw a table nearby (with only two free chairs; Guide stood behind us) with food on it. It was snack food: potato chips, pretzels, cookies, and such. Nobody looked at us, so we took some food and started listening. We heard this:

Blond-haired Woman: OK, I have my question. Why do little children suffer?

Brown-haired Woman: The single biggest reason is the shortage of resources. Scarcity forces some people groups to hoard food, medicine, and clothes, leaving others without enough to meet their needs. The solution is proper family management to keep the population from outgrowing available resources.

Old Man: And I would say that children suffer because large portions of the developed world do not realize how little material they need to live. With the proper education, rich countries would direct their technology to find ways to satisfy large populations with few resources. That technology, along with the material saved from the reduced demands of rich countries, could bring the whole world to a common, satisfactory standard. No more children would suffer.

Young Guy: OK, my turn. I look at it like this: The whole world is out of balance, right? And people out of balance do bad things, right? Because I think if you look real close, you'll see that most children's suffering is because of war. War is the problem; if we get rid of war by getting the world back in balance, then all children will be happy!

Blond-haired Woman: Wait a moment! I wasn't talking just about children in poverty or malnutrition, but all children everywhere who suffer. Why do *any* children suffer? Like children whose parents divorce, or who are abused, or . . .

At this point she trailed off, and the others didn't speak right away. Guide Girl tapped us both on the shoulder and motioned us to get up. When we stepped away from the table, she said, "Do you see how it works?"

"Works? You mean that was working? Someone asks an incredibly hard question and everyone else sounds off their opinions until they don't know what else to say?" Brad sounded unimpressed.

"Perhaps we left a bit early, but there is more to it than that. It goes like this: The Quester asks his Question, and then the Conversation begins. Everyone who has an answer proffers it in an abbreviated form. Then the Quester selects which answer will be developed and scrutinized first. Conversants cross-examine one another. Answers are weighed until the Quester becomes the Quaestor, at which point he judges which answer he will accept."

" 'Quester becomes the Quester'? What's that mean, and what's a quester in the first place?" He was still unimpressed.

"No, no; a *quester* becomes a *quaestor*. They are pronounced just alike, but you spell them differently, and they mean different things. A *quester* is one who goes on a quest, or search; in this case, a search for the answer to some important question. A *quaestor* is an official, like a judge or a government accountant."

Brad rolled his eyes, but I had to comment. "I see; you gather enough opinions to get your mind changed. No big swing, Dad would say. But it didn't seem to work like that back at that table, did it?"

"Ah, perhaps not, but it can take time." Guide looked down.

"Where'd that come from?" Brad asked. He was looking at my chest. A nametag had appeared there. It said *Quester.* I looked at Guide for an explanation.

"You are a Quester now," she said, as if it were obvious.

"Oh yeah? And what question do I ask?"

"What question got you here in the first place?"

I got her point, I think, and looked around for another table.

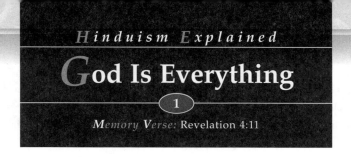

There was a table with two empty chairs close to us. I didn't see any other free chairs, so I headed that way. I tried to be nice and offer Guide Girl a seat, but she said that would be silly because I was the Quester. Then Brad dramatically offered her his seat, asking if he couldn't please show the courtesy that my status didn't allow, or something like that. I think he was actually surprised when she thanked him and sat down beside me, leaving him standing behind us alone.

As I looked around the table, my stomach tightened. They were a tough-looking group, and they were all looking tough at *me*. I don't mean tough in the beat-you-up sense, but tough as in smart. Suddenly I couldn't say anything.

Thankfully, one of them spoke up and said, "Welcome, Quester. We've been waiting for you. Make yourself comfortable, and have some cookies. Tea? Coffee? Water? Protein blaster? Jack, hand the kid a blaster. All right then, let me introduce myself and my colleagues. I'm Ted, this is Carla, that's Li, he's Ravi, and right here is

Jack. We're here to answer your Question. We have different ways of looking at things, but we can't all be right—at least, I don't think so. You'll get a spectrum of views. You'll come away with the truth, assuming you are perceptive enough to tell which answer is the best. Whenever you're ready, go ahead and ask away."

Ted was a white man, about forty years old. Carla was also white and not quite that old. Li was something like thirty and looked Chinese. Ravi was older than Ted, and looked like an Indian—from India, like Guide, not a Native American. Jack was a black man about the same age as Ravi and looked like an American. All of them were looking at me and waiting.

Now it occurred to me I hadn't worded a question yet. Thinking as I spoke, I asked, "What is there beyond what we can see?" Expecting a torrent of opinions, I waited.

"Plumbing."

"Air."

"Infrared light."

"Antarctica."

"The far side of the moon."

"Happiness."

Great. This may be harder than I thought. "I didn't mean like that."

"Then perhaps you need a more precise question." This was from Jack, who had a really deep, rich voice like you'd expect from a king or an opera singer. He was smiling at me. *Right, a more precise question.*

"OK. What is the ultimate, absolute truth? Is it God, or infinity, or enlightenment, or what? What's the one thing that matters more than anything else? What would still exist even if everything else was gone?"

That did it! They all grinned, or nodded, or took a breath. Then they gave me their short answers, one by one.

Ted led off. "God is the ideal that dwells in all of us, ever learning, growing, and changing. God is the projection of what we want to become. The personal God is the ideal individual, and the Absolute Oneness is the ideal corporate humanity. My colleagues will speak of God and the Oneness, but I maintain that what is truly real is yourself, Quester. You can always be sure that you exist, that your thoughts and dreams are real, and that the vision you have for your own future is the real hope of humanity."

Next spoke Carla. "Your question is simply beyond what human beings can know. Every answer to that question has been a human invention. Most of those have resulted in the enslavement of people to an impossible ideal, often at the hands of an elite who used such ideals to secure their own comfort and power. We cannot fall prey to the inventions of individuals, for each of us perceives reality through

an individual grid. I cannot claim that what is true for me is true for you. But what we can be sure of is our community, and the love and fulfillment of friendships with one another despite our diversity."

Li was number three. "I think God is the common name for something that goes by many different names. It is that which lies behind and stands above all that is, and is yet the total of all, though more than the mere sum of all things combined. From it we all come, and by finding ourselves we return there, though we never truly left it. By looking deep within, we realize that all we call 'real' is really illusion that masks the reality. When you ascend above the illusion of what you call 'real,' you will see the Oneness as it truly is, and then you will know what is truly real."

Ravi continued the opening. "My colleague Li has spoken well, though I suggest that his other beliefs may contradict his words. Indeed, there is one reality. He is all, and all is He. However, the life a mortal man leads is mired in the hardships born of iniquity past. By overcoming what is bad and embracing what is good, a man may transcend the bonds of life and find that he is part of that glorious one reality, God."

Jack spoke last. "God is the ultimate reality. He is the uncreated Creator of all else. He is innately good; goodness draws its very definition from His nature. He is perfect in respect to eternity, immensity, knowledge, being, and power. Everything in every order of reality was made by Him, all of it serves His purposes, and all of it exists for His ultimate glory and joy."

Then they all looked at me again. "OK. Thanks, everybody."

"You're supposed to choose one to hear and evaluate first," Guide Girl whispered, as if I should have remembered.

"Well, Brad and I were just talking about enlightenment, and the elevation of the spirit, and all that, so why don't we talk about that first?" I looked at Ravi, and he smiled.

"It is my honor. Please, would you like some tea?" They were passing fancy teacups around the table and pouring tea out of a shiny metal pot. I'm not big on tea (and I hadn't finished my protein blaster), but I took some. Be polite, Mom always says. The stuff tasted like grass.

Then Ravi began. "You have chosen to hear first about the world of the Hindu. You have wisely chosen the wellspring of religion as the beginning of your journey. All young people should take time for religion; it is not a matter to dismiss lightly. Let us begin.

"All the universe is a mosaic of immeasurable beauty. Outward it stretches in all directions, never repeating, yet never ending, made more and more beautiful by its scope of variety. Inward it penetrates to levels smaller than eyes see, things often similar yet never the same, beautiful in their shape, color, and activities. In all these there is music—a harmony of function, a melody of spirits, and the rhythm of life always new. All these dance together in the Great Dance. Time does not bound this Dance any more than death can end it. All that we call the universe could pass away, and still the Dance would continue.

All that we call the universe could pass away, and still the Dance would continue.

"Simple, though of utmost importance, is this fact: all of the universe, all of every universe, is in truth the same. All are One. Not one in form, but one in essence. And the One is conscious, living, breathing the breath of transcendent life; for being the totality of all things, it is more than all things. From that Oneness men come, and back to it they must go if they are to have eternal, infinite bliss.

"The process of bir—"

"Hold it! Hold it a minute," Brad interrupted. "First things first. How do you know all this? Who says this?"

"Holy men, too humble to record their names, who through patience and piety learned truth from the Brahman."

"From whom?"

"The Brahman is not *whom* as you are accustomed to using the word. Brahman is the Oneness, the totality of which all things are parts. The Brahman has been manifested at different times and in different ways; some of the holy writers were appearances of him in human form, it seems."

"Him? But you said Brahman is not *whom."*

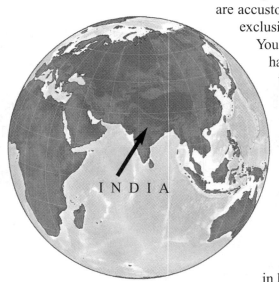

I N D I A

"Some things are unclear because you are accustomed to using language exclusively instead of inclusively. You must rise above that habit, which is caused by the *maya,* the illusion of this world. The Brahman is neither it nor he, as you are accustomed to think of those words. Brahman is both at once, and therefore your pronouns are inadequate without deeper insight.

"Perhaps I should cover in brief the history of Indian

religion. Long ago the Vedas were given to man; given by God, as you might hear it said. There are four Vedas. Three are older than men can reckon, and the fourth appeared in ancient times. These holy scriptures predate any other religious texts and give the kernel of truth that points the way to enlightenment. They are beautiful hymns and incantations concerning the ritual of sacrifice. They give the first known revelation of the truth that all is One.

"The Vedas themselves are somewhat difficult to understand, especially for the modern mind. More accessible are their Upanishads, the commentaries written by great teachers to explain the Vedas. The Upanishads first expound the doctrine of *karma,* the principle that what one does in one life affects his next life. Karma results in a process of reincarnation through which a being passes on its journey to reunification with the Brahman.

"The Upanishads appeared some 2500 years ago, and it is important to realize that during the following centuries India was not a land of one religion but of many, as it is today. There has never been a single correct way of Hinduism. Hinduism is by definition a collection of ways, all of which lead ultimately to the same place, though some speed the journey more than others do. Indian

Sanskrit

Sanskrit is one of the most ancient languages still studied today. It was developed in India and was used to write the Vedas, the oldest Hindu texts. From Sanskrit, the formal language, came many *Prakrits* or local, informal dialects. It also gave rise to the Indo-Aryan language family. The preservation of Hindu writings, both scriptures and commentaries on them, helped to preserve Sanskrit even to this day. Below is a Sanskrit sample from the *Dictionary of Languages.* (Andrew Dalby, *Dictionary of Languages* [New York: Columbia UP, 1998], 538–40.)

वाशीमेको बिभर्ति हस्त आयसीमन्तर्देवेषु निधुविः

One's hand holds an adze of iron, working amid the gods.

religions were developing with the times and were far ahead of other faiths, even in the centuries just prior to the Christian era in the West. For example, it was during this time that Brahmins, Indian religious leaders, first elaborated the doctrine of the *ashrams,* or stages of life, explaining that a person must grow in successive stages in order to escape karma and ascend to the Oneness.

"A major advance in Indian religion occurred at the same time as the rise of Christianity. It is signified by the writing of the Mahabharata, chief of the great epics. At the heart of the Mahabharata is the Bhagavad-Gita, the single most important religious text of India. In that text, the god Krishna explains in dialogue with the human hero of the epic, Arjuna, the importance of duty, spiritual discipline, and devotion. These three things are the ways to liberation from karma and exaltation to the realm of divinity."

Guide Girl spoke up. "Perhaps, Ravi, you could explain the significance of the epic? It isn't familiar to Americans and other westerners how epics can be major religious texts."

"Yes, yes, epics. There is no better way to learn about Hinduism than simply to read the great epics of India. Perhaps it seems odd to you to think of epics as spiritual scriptures, but if you pause to consider, you may realize it isn't so far removed from your own experience. For example, the Christian Bible contains epic stories with which it teaches lessons about God and man, such as the story of the Exodus of Israel from Egypt.

"Furthermore, you must not think of the epics as dogmatic or infallible. They are the unfolding of absolute truth, but they do not reveal the whole of what a man can learn of truth, nor will they teach the same lessons to every man. There are other great epics, notably the Ramayana; the Mahabharata is only the best known and most widely respected. The epics teach truth; they are not truth themselves. They are communication of truth through artistry, a replication of human experience so that we can relate truth more easily to our own experiences.

"Moving along, I wish to emphasize that during what you would call the Middle Ages, there was development in Hindu understanding of the gods. Krishna has also the name Vishnu, and many Hindus worship the god Vishnu as the embodiment of the supreme reality. Yet the most popular is the god Shiva, frequent champion of the epics and the most thoroughly comprehensive representation of the great Oneness, in the opinion of many Hindus.

"The popular texts that serve as scripture to the average Hindu appeared at this same time. They are called the Puranas. Some are devoted to exalting one god, either Brahma, Vishnu, or Shiva, and others exalt multiple gods. The content of the Puranas makes Hinduism what it is in the minds of many. Now that I have told you in brief of the rise of Hinduism, I will return to the elaboration of Hindu beliefs.

"As I was saying, the process of birth, life, death, and rebirth is karma, the cycle from which we must be freed in order to become one with the All. A good life is rewarded with rebirth into a better state, and a bad life results in rebirth into a lower state. It is possible to ascend even to the realm of the gods for a season. It is also possible to descend into the places of torment, if one does great evil in a lifetime."

It is possible to ascend even to the realm of the gods for a season.

"What do you consider evil?" I wondered.

"Evil is selfishness, cruelty, greed, jealousy, and all the things men everywhere know to be wrong. All of it comes from the failure to realize that what is seen is illusion, and what is true is beyond all that can be seen with the eyes. Man must realize that he is part of the infinite soul and endowed with unbounded potential. Only then will he realize the worthlessness of sins and rise above them to take his seat in the heavens."

"Is this what all Hindus believe?" I asked.

"As I said, Hinduism is not one belief. Many beliefs were born in India over the years. Religion is India's gift to the world. What you call Hinduism is a broad canopy encompassing many faiths, many systems. These are beautiful in their diversity and beautiful in their kernel of unity. All share the beliefs I have told you, though their particular emphasis, or ceremony, or legends, or the name by which they call their god or gods differ."

Brad leaned over the table between Carla and Ted. "But they all have common scriptures, right? They all believe these Vedas, and epics, and Puranas, and the other things you said. Isn't that right?"

"Not exactly. What you mean by *scriptures* cannot be taken too narrowly. There are many paths to the one goal, and naturally different scriptures mean different things to the spiritually minded. One Hindu sect may reject part or even all of one or more holy writings without losing the essence of Hinduism. But I will tell you of the holy—"

"Excuse me, but why are there so many different ways and religions, and why would the same scriptures mean different things to different people?" Brad was serious for once. "I realize I'm using words all the wrong way and not thinking openly enough, but I'm sure you understand." Serious, but still Brad.

"Certainly," Ravi answered him. "A very good question. A natural question many westerners ask. But let me first draw attention to the great diversity in your own religious heritage. How many major denominations of Christianity are there? And within those, how many minor variations, down to shades of difference so slight no one outside can tell the difference? All these are in your heritage, all called by the same name and sharing unity amid diversity. Therefore, it is no peculiarity of Hinduism that there is a plurality of viewpoints.

"Now as to the reason for differences, as you asked. As I see it, the primary reason is that people are different from one another. Different people require different approaches to religion. Your needs may differ from mine; consequently, your religious preferences may differ. To each, the path that is most suitable serves best. After all, karma is not the same to all men at birth, and that is why we see men born into vastly different conditions."

"Karma—that's what makes people be reincarnated, right?"

"To be precise, karma is the law governing the cycle of rebirths through which one must pass to overcome the illusion of the world. The life one leads determines what sort of life one will enter next. Eventually, one can break the cycle by reaching reunion with the Oneness."

"OK, now this I've heard about," Brad interjected. "That's the same as enlightenment, when the world just falls away and you enter a higher spiritual plane. You suddenly see everything as it really is, and then you go into heaven, or nirvana, or whatever."

THE BRAHMAN

THE PLACES OF TORMENT

"Very good! All of that is true. However, you are using the term that my colleague Li would choose instead of the one I would choose. Li will say that an earthly man can reach enlightenment, as Buddhists believe. But what I speak of—ultimate re-unification with the absolute One—is not for a man who walks the earth, but for one who has ascended above the illusion of life. *Nirvana* is also a Buddhist term, but it more closely represents what I speak of.

Man is part of all that is, and all that is is Brahman.

"Yet to truly understand, you must understand what union with the Oneness *is.* Man is part of all that is, and all that is is Brahman. Different Hindus use different names for him and stress different parts of his personality; some call him God Shiva, some call him God Vishnu, some stress more of his own actions and less of his identity with all the rest of the universe. Nevertheless, all Hindus refer to the Oneness. I call the Oneness Brahman, its old and revered name.

"Thus man is part of all, and all is Brahman, and therefore man is really Brahman. That truth is obscured by the illusion, but when the illusion is cast away, man becomes again part of the Oneness by realizing that he is indeed part of the One. This is the ascent to the divine."

A pause followed as we digested all of this stuff. Brad was the first to speak again. "OK, interesting. Have you ever reached enlightenment, or re-union, or whatever you call it?"

Ravi laughed. "No, or else I would not be here. As I said, a man of earth cannot have been liberated from illusion. I have meditated and exercised and gained great awareness, but I am yet a pilgrim to the Oneness."

"Do you know anybody who has gotten there?"

"Of course not! Only the gods and the holy ones have come from the Oneness to tell us the way of truth. Such as have returned to the All are now part of the Brahman, whether he acts as God Shiva or God Vishnu or under any other name, and therefore they are in that sense active in guiding us to the absolute. They are no longer persons as you and I."

"In that case, how am I supposed to know it's the truth? You say all this about moving up through karma to get back in touch with the Oneness, and it sounds good, but how do I really know it's like that?"

"Ultimately, Brad, the proof of what I say lies buried inside you, waiting to be unearthed. There is more than one way to reach inside and find it, but if you seek it you will find it. Do you not sense a unity with other people, as well as with all life, and nature, and the cosmos above? Do you not have a sense that you are far more than you appear? Do you not have dreams and desires that transcend the commonplace existence thrust upon us all? That is from the essence of Oneness within you. You may call it the seed of the divine, or even the presence of God.

"What I have told you is the essence of the richest and deepest religious heritage on earth. You are privileged to enjoy the cream of over three thousand years' work. Some 800 million people are Hindus, and the number grows rapidly. Inclusive, optimistic, spiritually satisfying, mentally satisfying—that is Hinduism, and that is why it is the apex of human religion!"

To Hindus, Shiva's dance expresses his power as creator, preserver, and destroyer of the universe.

"All right, time for a snack!" Li, the Chinese guy, stood up, and everyone else did too. We went over to the wall where several snack machines and refrigerators stood. As everyone got something to chew (Li handed me these fruit-bar-like things), Guide Girl asked me what I thought so far.

"I think the Hinduism stuff is neat. That's all cool to know. But what now? Do I pick somebody else to do the same thing?"

"Yes, you will select the next one to present an answer. But first there must be the interrogation. Each conversant cross-examines the speaker with a single question. The speaker answers, but only you may ask follow-up questions, so if you think the speaker avoided the question or failed to answer well enough, you have to pursue it yourself. After all four of the others have asked and received answers, you can select another speaker. Of course, there will probably have to be a cake break first."

"Cake break?"

"Surely. Thinking is hard work, you know. It takes lots of energy to maintain."

Hard work. Right. Well, I do always come home from school hungry. I hoped the cake would be good, because my fruit bars had been boring.

We were still getting settled when Ted launched into the question time. "All right, tell me this," he said. "What good has Hinduism done for people over three thousand years? The people of India or anywhere else—have they lived better under Hinduism? Has it led to advances in technology or a broader understanding of the physical world? Has it cured diseases, or fed the hungry, or in any substantial way boosted the quality of life of the millions who live under it? I don't think it has. Isn't India today saddled with poverty, malnutrition, sickness, and people trapped in their stations of life with no way to better themselves? In fact, hasn't India's entire history been one long Dark Age?"

I leaned over to Guide. "I thought he got to ask just one question."

"That was just one question," she whispered back. "His first question was the main question. The rest just clarified it and reinforced it."

"Oh." I looked at Ravi. He looked tolerant, nodding slightly as if this were nothing new to him. He took a slow breath and began, his voice as even as it had been before.

Hindu peoples have always partaken of physical pleasures.

"It is a common fallacy that Hindu religions scorn material matters. The truth is that Hindu peoples have always partaken of physical pleasures, recognizing the proper use of physical things. It was the task of three of the four traditional castes to deal with the material world for the benefit of society; laborers worked, merchants traded, and warriors fought. These tasks continue today with the full approval of the clergy. The proper utilization of material things is thus a part of Hinduism.

OK, first he said that you get to heaven by realizing that the world isn't real; now he says Hindus utilize material things—"But didn't you say that the way for anyone to move closer to Brahman is to get away from the real world, or the material world, and realize that it is all illusion?"

"Certainly," Ravi replied, rocking slightly in his chair. "But as long as so many are trapped in illusion, it is obviously necessary to utilize—"

"The illusion?" Brad supplied.

"To utilize what is needful to sustain life until enough can be learned to transcend karma and advance to a higher plane." Ravi glanced at Brad with a slight smile.

Guide Girl spoke. "Excuse me, sir, but before we are side-tracked and you are kept from finishing your answer to Ted's question, could you address whether or not his allegation is true? Do Indian people really live as he described?"

"It is true, tragically, that many people in India have suffered greatly. But this is not due to their beliefs. First, the worst deprivations have resulted from war, as they always do. Poor India has been invaded and enslaved by outside powers repeatedly throughout its history. Atrocity and repression inevitably lower the standard of living." Ravi's mouth smiled here, but his eyes didn't.

"Second, many Indians voluntarily choose to live ascetically for the sake of purifying their souls, focusing on the spiritual, and unburdening others of competition for wealth. This is not integral to all Hindu beliefs, but it can hardly be termed a Dark Age. Could it not be that your Western conception of progress and success as defined by material accumulated is the real oppressor? Is it so hard to believe someone might choose to live without electronics, and cars, and huge but empty mansions?"

Guide Girl spoke again. "Thank you very much. Please allow me to ask another question for the sake of clarity. If I may presume so much, I will restate Ted's question as a syllogism."

"A whatogism?" I asked, then felt stupid because everyone looked away while Guide explained it to me.

"A syllogism is a logical construct consisting of three statements: two propositions and a conclusion. To be valid, or logical, the conclusion has to follow logically from the premises. Anything that is logical can be expressed as a syllogism. Here, let me restate what Ted asked, and see if I get it right.

"Ted implied that poverty and malnutrition are bad. He assumed that whatever causes poverty and malnutrition is bad. It may seem obvious, but that was his first premise: Anything that causes poverty and malnutrition is bad. His second premise was that Hinduism causes poverty and malnutrition. His conclusion is that therefore Hinduism is bad. Now Ravi, obviously, must refute one or both premises in order to refute the conclusion. Ravi, you seem to have struck at both, but maybe not specifically enough for the sake of us students. Could you please respond to each premise again?"

Whatever causes poverty and malnutrition is bad.

Hinduism causes poverty and malnutrition.

Hinduism is bad.

I saw Ted smirk. I thought Jack smiled, but just a little.

"Gladly," Ravi said, leaning forward. "Poverty is wrong when it is involuntary or when it causes suffering. Malnutrition is likewise wrong due to the suffering it causes. I do not deny that the living conditions of many Hindus are deplorable. Therefore, I agree that whoever inflicts deprivation and suffering upon others is wrong.

"But the suggestion that Hinduism is to blame for the suffering of India is preposterous. As I said, outside invaders are to blame. Wars, selfishness, thievery, and greed are the reasons, not religion, except a religion that teaches men to harm others!

"Admittedly, sometimes the perpetrator is a Hindu. Many who go by the name of Hindu live far short of Hindu ideals; others act in outright contradiction to them. Just because one man wrongs another man and both are what you would call Hindus does not mean Hindu religions cause suffering."

I thought about that for a second, thinking about something Ravi said earlier, something about people suffering. Something just didn't seem to match. "Hey, Ravi, didn't you say earlier that people suffer in this life for what they did wrong in a previous life?"

"Yeah," Brad chimed in. "Do people in India suffer because of what they did wrong or what someone else did wrong? I mean, wouldn't it be true that Indian people suffer because they were evil in their former lives?"

Ravi looked down and back up. "Karma ensures that everyone receives the just result of his previous life. Those who suffer at the hands of others do so, at least in part, because of karma from a past life. Those who wrong them, even though they be the agents of karma, will likewise face retribution in their own following lives."

Karma ensures that everyone receives the just result of his previous life.

Everyone got quiet while I digested Ravi's last statement. It seemed to fit, but there was something nagging me I couldn't quite reach . . . Ah! "Ravi, if karma always has to come from a past life, how did it get started in the first place?"

"The universe goes through cycles of dissolution and restoration. It is the way of things."

Well, now they were all looking at me again, Jack especially hard, I thought, but Li looked like he was going to burst, so I nodded to him.

Li began by complimenting Ravi, going on about the rich heritage of tradition among the religions of the East and how great it was to sit and talk about them. Li seemed happy and very eager, almost nervous. He sounded more American than Chinese and talked really fast.

"It's kind of a funny thing to Americans that Indian and Chinese religions, if I can generalize like that, seem so much alike. I won't deny that Buddhism has its roots in India. But there are differences, even though we would not dispute that there are different paths to absolute truth.

"However, I've got a question about the way Indian sages talk about reality and truth; why insist upon speaking as if your deity, or deities, were persons? Supposedly in your sacred texts they are both personal and not personal, I know, but doesn't that fact contradict our foundational belief that all is One? Hindu texts and modern teachings talk about God and spirit beings and demons, but don't those belong to the primitive religions? They sound more like the paganism of Europe and Africa and, yes, India. That's nothing but superstition, and it causes nothing but strife. Wouldn't Hindus be better off if they let go of the idea of divine beings and stick to the idea at the heart of their beliefs, that all is One?"

I couldn't sort out what Li meant, but Ravi answered like he was familiar with the question. "My Buddhist friend charges Hinduism with inconsistency, a crime of which Buddhism is no doubt innocent in his eyes. This takes us at once to the nature of the Supreme. Hindus have different views of the true nature of the Supreme, as I have said. But this is to be expected if he is infinite, absolute, transcendent, and in all other ways the ultimate that we can imagine. Different men will see different aspects of him.

"The Supreme Being—let us call it the God Shiva for the sake of speaking—is more than just the sum total of all that there is. He is more than the sum of everything added together. He is the living essence of all things and therefore in himself he is absolute truth. If the epics relate his speaking to a man, it is the same as if a man learned the truth that is behind all things, which is Shiva. That truth wants to be made known to men to liberate them from illusion and embrace them to itself, giving them liberty. Shiva is both everything and more than everything. How could an absolute God not be both at once? Just as the Jewish or Christian God is limited by being different from the universe, so your Buddhist atheism limits him by making him no more than the universe."

Now it was my turn to ask a question, but my head was kind of spinning. What should I ask Ravi now? Something was bothering me about what he had said, but with all of them looking at me again, especially the way Jack was squinting at me, I couldn't think straight. So I threw a lateral to Brad. "What do you think, Mr. Brilliant?"

"It seems like Ravi can agree that the Supreme Being is just about anything anyone claims he is. Is there anything you would say that the Supreme Being is *not?* For example, what about the spirit beings and demons? Are they part of him?"

"The Supreme Being is not badness, sorrow, or suffering. He is not hatred, greed, or malice. The spirit beings Li refers to are no less part of him than every star, every flower, and every human being is part of him. Some Hindus believe in what Li calls demons, true, but they are considered to be immature souls who are yet bound by a love of evil and illusion."

Brad had a look that meant he was skeptical of something. "So what causes evil things if they are not part of Shiva, but Shiva is everything that is? Where did evil come from if it isn't part of the Oneness?"

Ravi seemed undisturbed. "As I said, the universe goes through endless cycles. Karma is simply a fact. Shiva has not bothered to describe the beginning of karma as other than the beginning of a cycle."

It seemed like a good time for the next question, so I told Carla to go ahead.

"Thank you!" she said, with this really sweet smile. "I'd be happy to ask Ravi a question. Let me say first that I appreciate his attitude and his courtesy.

"But as for my question, I have to say—and I guess I'm echoing Li here—that Hinduism has got to admit that a lot of things in its past were just not appropriate. Don't get me wrong; Hinduism has a lot of good things to offer, and many Hindus have been very good people who did great things for their fellow human beings. Gandhi, for one, Mahatma Gandhi, I recognize as a man who really cared to improve the condition of everybody, especially the poor people and the oppressed. And he didn't believe in violence as a way to solve problems. He changed people's minds by setting a personal example.

"So there is plenty of good in Hinduism, but like Gandhi I'd have to identify a core of good ideas in the middle of a lot of bad ideas that have accumulated over the centuries as people used Hinduism to secure their own power. I don't think they are the real heart of Hinduism, but Hinduism has got to look forward to a better way and get rid of its outmoded ideological baggage."

"Is there a question coming soon?" Ravi smiled good-naturedly.

"Oh, I'm sorry, and I didn't mean that last sentence to be too harsh, but really it is my question. I guess my question is, Are you willing to say that Hinduism needs to denounce some things in its past and move forward toward a new understanding of the human condition?

"For example, do you admit to the oppression of women in the name of Hinduism throughout India's history? Not that Hinduism was really to blame, but that Hindu religious leaders oppressed women's rights just like the leaders of every other major religion in world history. And will you agree that the cosmology you claim underlies the universe cannot really be verified?"

"Whoa! What in the world is *cosmalology?*" I asked.

"Cosmology," Carla corrected me. "It's the branch of study dealing with the origin and order of the universe. Anyway, what I was asking was, Isn't it true, Ravi, that your cosmology has been used by the Brahmins to secure their own power and prestige, oppressing the masses under them who were not lucky enough to be born into a Brahmin family? I mean, Gandhi took that stand. Don't you think all Indians, and all Hindus, need to take the same stand?"

Ravi rocked back in his chair. "If I understand you correctly, you want me to admit that elements of historical Hinduism are inappropriate to today's values. I believe I have already indicated an awareness of that fact. I have also pointed out that much evil done in the name of Hinduism has been in conflict with its ideals.

"I would add that your question, Carla, borders on conflict with your own views. Are you not taking it upon yourself to impose morality on previous generations by assuming that their society was unjust? I don't wish to defend the abuses of historic Hinduism, but merely to observe that we cannot fully identify with their situation and should not, therefore, presume to judge them too harshly."

I had to think for a minute before asking a question. "Ravi, you're saying that oppressing women may have been wrong and it may not have been, and that bossing other people around may have been wrong and it may not have been—you can see it either way?"

"*Oppressing* and *bossing* are wrong in the way you mean them. But what constitutes *oppressing* and *bossing* is a harder question. And the point is that you can't blame Hinduism for them, anyway." Ravi sounded a little bit mad, but I guess I could see why.

What constitutes oppressing and bossing is a harder question.

"Ravi," Guide Girl said, "Carla asked whether or not the cosmology of Hinduism can be verified. You don't have to address that if you don't want to, because it really was another question, but if there is anything you want to say to that point I know we would like to hear it."

"The proof of the Supreme Oneness lies within us. I see no reason to say more than that."

Guide looked at me now and said, "Do you have any other follow-up questions for Ravi?"

"No, I guess not. Maybe we ought to take a break before Jack asks his question?" I thought Ravi might want a break. Guide seemed to think this was out of order, but everyone else jumped right up and headed for the refreshment wall. Nobody got any food, but they all got a drink of water or orange juice and stretched. I saw Ravi get a big cup of water and drink it without talking to anyone. Li and Carla chattered about something I couldn't follow.

As everyone settled down again, Jack looked at me with a *Well?* look and I just nodded to him. He turned to Ravi and said this: "Since we are speaking for the benefit of these young people, I would like to ask for a clarification." Jack's voice was deep and nice to listen to, like he must have been a good singer or could record books on tape. "Let us suppose that I am a man who comes to you guilt-ridden over my sins and frustrated with the hardships of life. All I want is to be certain of a better world to come after this life is over. I will do anything necessary to reach such a world if only someone shows me how. What would you tell me?"

Beatles singer George Harrison (in black) was a westerner who promoted Hare Krishna's "peace without guilt" philosophy in his song lyrics.

Ravi laughed at that a little, like he was surprised, or maybe relieved. "Perhaps I would first tell you to let go of the baggage of Christian society that lays guilt on your shoulders and tricks you into believing you must always have more and more material things to be happy. But I would certainly teach you that the hardships of this life are due to the limitations of the physical body. The world we see and all its suffering is but illusion. That is the first truth I would teach you, Jack, and it would free your heart.

"As for reaching a better world beyond this life—something we all seek—" (Ted snorted here) "I would assure you that not only is such a world possible, but that it is the ultimate destiny of all souls. The right kind of life now, one free of selfishness and hatred and violence, can set you on a permanent journey through higher and higher spiritual planes, to better and better worlds, until you are one with Shiva."

Ravi leaned back and thought for a second. "I take time with every neophyte to teach appropriate acts of devotion. What acts are appropriate can change with every person, so I would have to talk with you at length to find out which would be best for you. Piety has many forms of expression, perhaps an infinite number. They are both external and internal, but all serve the same purpose of purifying the soul and bringing it into unity with the Brahman."

Then Brad asked, "So is that the bottom line? Lighten up, be good, smoke a pipe, or whatever, and go to heaven? If I were the neophyte, I could do that and be sure I would go to heaven?" (By the way, a *neophyte* is someone who is new at something. I had to ask Guide Girl about that during the next break. I think it's a cool word.)

"Yes, in fact, that is the bottom line."

"So do you know for a fact that you are going on to heaven?" Brad continued.

"*Heaven* is your word. Notice, Brad, that even Jack did not say *heaven,* but 'a better world.' I would reserve *heaven* for that point at which I will be blissfully united with Shiva. I do not know that that will come in my next life, but I can be sure that a good life now can set me on a permanent course of progress through better worlds that will eventually lead me to that point."

"OK, then you are at least sure your next life will be better than this one?"

"I have every reason to believe I have fulfilled karma in this life and will therefore ascend to a better life." Brad didn't ask anything else. I would like to have had a brilliant question to finish this round with, but it's hard to think on your feet. Besides, I needed another break and something better to eat than those fruit things.

People were pushing back their chairs for yet another break until I spoke up. "Wait a minute." Hesitation. "Jack, why did you ask what you did, that imaginary guilt situation?"

"Imaginary?" Jack looked me in the eye. "The situation I used was hypothetical, but even Ravi would agree that the fact of guilty feelings is no stretch of the imagination." Ravi bobbed his head as if he agreed with the idea but was uneasy about where it might lead. Jack went on, "If everything is One, and changeless karma is supreme, then there is no outside standard to judge right and wrong. Ravi would be right in saying guilt is needless."

"But I thought Ravi said Shiva, not karma, was the Supreme Oneness," Brad inserted. Jack looked at Ravi as if to say, *Well?*

Ravi made a broad gesture. "We are too much in the illusion to know all about how karma and Shiva relate. . . . I do think the mystery is wrapped up in the Oneness of things."

Hindu yogis chant the symbol Om (pronounced ō-m) to connect to the One Reality it represents.

Jack shook his head. "Ravi, that's what you said a minute ago. But there's the rub. Which is supreme? Karma or Shiva? The problem of guilt and evil must be dealt with somehow. You can place it with karma, but that means that Shiva, your Supreme Oneness, is neither supreme nor one. He is not supreme because he is subject to karma; he cannot help the evil it produces. Nor is he one, since there is something outside of him. If you insist that Shiva is in fact the Supreme Oneness, then you must leave the problem of evil with him. But if you do that, then either your god is evil, or else evil is non-existent—just another part of the Oneness. But you say *you* are a part of Shiva too. How can a supreme and unified being forget himself, much less adopt a view of guilt and evil that goes against his own nature?"

Brad grunted in disgust. "So in the end, this whole thing ends up giving us a universe without a Supreme Being, or else I wind up as part of a Supreme Being who's *really* messed up." He got up and headed for the snack area, tossing over his shoulder, "Thanks for making me a part of this."

Everything Is Nothing

3

The cake break turned out to be pretty good. They had five different kinds of "cake." There were tube-like things with chocolate icing and chocolate filling, little squares of white cake with pink icing all over that tasted like mint and strawberry, and round flat things with a sort of bitter powder on top. There was also some weird brown stuff with a sharp, fruity taste, and finally a plain yellow-colored cake that was unbelievably moist and good. I found out later that these were the favorites of each of the five talkers. Jack's was the plain yellow one, which he called "pound cake." Those brainy types really know how to snack!

Anyway, we sat back down and I was supposed to pick the next person. I thought back to what they'd all said at the beginning. I remembered how Ravi and Li had talked about having similar ideas and how they'd talked to each other later, polite but pointed. I figured I should hear Li while Ravi was still fresh in my mind so I could see just how much they had in common.

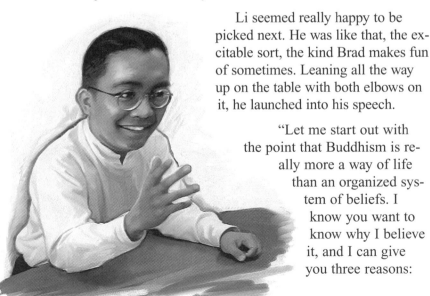

Li seemed really happy to be picked next. He was like that, the excitable sort, the kind Brad makes fun of sometimes. Leaning all the way up on the table with both elbows on it, he launched into his speech.

"Let me start out with the point that Buddhism is really more a way of life than an organized system of beliefs. I know you want to know why I believe it, and I can give you three reasons:

the testimony of people who experienced enlightenment for themselves, the long-established presence of Buddhism around the world, and my innate sense of truth that is so drawn toward Buddhism. But the fact is that Buddhism is all about why life is like it is, and how we should live it. You know what I mean? No matter who you are or where you are, you need to know how to live, right? All right then, here we go.

"Buddhism doesn't have an absolute beginning, because it's always been the truth, but its big advance came from the life of Siddhartha Gautama, a great teacher who lived in northern India about 2500 years ago. He lived in a time when India was a mess of competing religions—no offense, dude," (this was directed to Ravi, who nodded tolerantly)—"and people were really searching for the truth.

"Gautama was like a prince, born into a noble family, the oldest son and heir to his family's land and title. Some wise men had prophesied at his birth that he would either be a worldwide king or a Buddha, a great religious figure. Because his father wanted him to become a king, he sheltered him and pampered him like you wouldn't believe, so much so that he apparently rarely, if ever, saw anyone suffer. But that changed as he grew up.

"Gautama was out one day with his chariot driver and saw an old, broken-down man shuffling along the roadside. Another day he saw a very sick man lying by the road. Finally he saw a dead body. It struck Gautama that a lot of people were really bad off, always sick, poor, and suffering. Not only that, but he realized that everybody in the world is bound to end up old, sick, and eventually dead. Probably he had been aware of suffering before, but later he said that seeing those people on the road made him start his search for truth.

"He gave up his fortune and his title and went looking for teachers who could show him the meaning of life and the reason for so much suffering. He even had to leave his wife and newborn child. His family, including his wife, thought he had gone totally nuts. It must have been amazingly hard for him to begin his quest with so much opposition."

He realized that everybody in the world is bound to end up old, sick, and eventually dead.

"Do you suppose it was at all hard on his wife?" Guide Girl asked nicely.

"Sure, but Gautama was drawn by a longing for higher truth. Besides, his wife comes back into the story later on." Li resettled himself. "Anyway, Gautama studied under a couple of teachers and learned everything they knew, but he still hadn't reached absolute truth. So he tried several years of what they call 'self-mortification,' meaning basically that he tried to do without food. But that got him nothing but sick and skinny."

I asked why Gautama had thought starving would help in the first place. "It was popular to think that denying the body like that—depriving it of food, or sleep, or good clothes, or whatever—made you more spiritual. You know—if the body is illusion, rubbing it out should stop the illusion. So if riches didn't enlighten, and poverty didn't enlighten, he would take the Middle Path between them—neither overrich nor overpoor." Here Li glanced at Ravi but didn't say anything to him. "Anyway, asceticism didn't work, so Gautama started eating again."

"I was going to say Buddha always looks pudgy in pictures," Brad remarked. Li ignored him and continued.

"Not long afterward, after he had been working for a while at meditating to gain enlightenment, he sat down, determined not to get up until he succeeded. And he did! The story goes that he fought a battle with the tempter god Mara and all his demons of passion, overcoming them with the Ten Virtues gained in his past lives."

"Demons of passion?" Brad asked, befuddled.

"Ten Virtues from past lives?" I asked, equally befuddled.

"Yeah. Sorry, I'm getting there. Mara is the force of desire in the world, the root of all suffering."

"But Buddhism doesn't have individual gods and demons like that, like Hinduism does. You said so," Brad pointed out.

"Right. Mara is not actually another being, he's a—what do you call it? When you talk about something like it's a person, but it's not."

"Personification?" Carla offered.

"Yeah! Mara is the personification of the force of passion. The word means 'illusion' and is used there for a being that embodies the idea. One interpretation in Buddhism is that Mara is a person who actually earned his status as a god by being good and got the privilege of using temptation to purify others. But I just usually think of it as symbolic language. It's like Gautama fought with and overcame evil within himself. He finally conquered all of his own passions. That enabled him to rise above the world and finally see things as they really, really are. He gained enlightenment!"

"But those virtues from past lives, what was that about?"

"Oh! Those were the virtues, the good character traits, that he had perfected during his past lives. They came to the surface that night to overcome Mara."

"So Buddhists believe in reincarnation, just like Hindus?"

"Right. Well, not exactly like Hindus, but we certainly believe beings move through different cycles in the endless chain of being. Gautama, in his previous lives, had accumulated all the traits necessary to become enlightened. That's what *buddha* means—Enlightened One. That's why we call him *the* Buddha, because it means 'the Enlightened One.' "

"Was Gautama the first Buddha?" Guide Girl wanted to know.

"No. He said that, in a past life, he had met the previous Buddha and from him had determined to become a Buddha. He also supposedly met the next Buddha just before entering the world for the last time. When, one day far into the future, Buddhism has been lost again, the next Buddha will come to earth and reach enlightenment—just like Gautama did—and then he'll teach everyone the truth again. Pretty cool, huh?"

"Wow," said Brad. "So, Buddhism isn't really a new religion, but a rediscovered one? There used to be Buddhists before Buddha, and there will be more Buddhists later who follow a different Buddha?"

"Yeah, that's right! Over time, Mara gains a footing as the memories of truth fade, but always another Buddha is on the way. I like to think of it in a symbolic way, too: no matter how much damage is done as humans give in to their passions, the force of purifying goodness will always rebound to steer us toward en-lightenment."

"Do you think Hinduism and the other religions are a result of Mara gaining a footing?" Guide asked next.

"Well, no offense, but that's what the Buddha discovered. Not that you can't find truth without calling yourself a Buddhist. All religions go in the same general direction, and all have some of the same ethics and morals."

All religions go in the same general direction, and all have some of the same ethics and morals.

I wanted to hear the rest of Gautama's story. "Was Buddha, or Gautama, born knowing that he was going to become Buddha? You said he left home wandering, looking for the truth. But if he'd had all those previous lives, why didn't he remember?"

"There are some funny stories about his birth. For instance, he supposedly walked around and said something like 'I am the greatest being in the world' just after being born. But like with all religions, you can tell the difference between stories meant to make a point and stories meant to be taken literally.

"Anyway, no one knows his past lives when first born into the world, because the illusion of desires is so strong in children. But the previous lives are still there, or at least the thread of karma from past lives is there. When he reached enlightenment, Gautama gained the power to see all of his past lives. He gained the power to see past the illusion and see everything as it really is."

Brad cut in. "Could he see everyone else's past lives?"

"Yeah, actually, he could. He knew everything."

"Could he see everyone's future lives?" Guide followed.

"Well, yeah, I guess. I mean, he could tell the future about some things, though I don't remember his saying anywhere that he knew all about everyone's future lives. But he must have.

"The next thing I was going to say was, he really wrestled for a while with whether or not he should teach what he had learned, because people weren't ready to receive it. But he could see the future enough to know that a few people would. One was his wife. His wife became one of his followers. See, I told you she came back into the story."

"If enlightenment showed him everything, why did he have to wonder even for a moment whether or not he should teach? Didn't you say that he came to the world from his former life just to bring the truth to the world, and that at enlightenment he would have realized that too?" I asked.

Li thought for a moment. "Well, he didn't wonder for very long, and he did decide to teach. I think his hesitation was more like a lesson to the rest of us that we should appreciate what he was saying." No one asked another question, so Li resumed his presentation.

"The essence of the Buddha's teaching is the Four Noble Truths. They form a progressive outline of the problem of life and its solution. The Four Noble Truths are the fact of suffering, the solution to suffering, the existence of nirvana, and the way to nirvana. Let me go through them.

"First is the fact that suffering exists. This was what started Gautama on his quest, and it's what drives almost everyone to seek ultimate truth. The term he used was *dukkha,* and it means something like 'illusion,' or a thing that is temporary, rather than suffering. It's more accurate to say that dukkha is the cause of suffering. You see, everything is in a permanent state of change. Everything around us is always changing, and we ourselves are always changing. Think about it: we eat and drink constantly, and our bodies turn the food into body tissues to replace what is lost. Science has shown that Buddha was right by proving that our cells are constantly dying and being replaced. We have a completely new body about every seven or eight years!

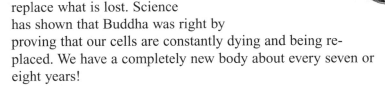

"Science has also backed up Buddha by showing that all physical matter is made up of particles in constant motion. Everything is always moving; nothing is the same from moment to moment or year to year. We see everything wear out, everyone get old; every living thing dies and every material thing decays."

"Your point is . . ." I had to ask.

"My point—really the Buddha's point—is that we have to escape constant change in order to have true bliss. As long as we live inside the illusion, we cannot be permanently happy. All kinds of things make us unhappy, including change itself. Change upsets our comfort and distresses our souls. Even happiness itself is ultimately a cause of suffering, because it can be lost, which is worse than never having been happy at all. So you see, everything is ultimately a source of suffering because everything is illusion. Don't think Buddhists are against being happy; Buddhism encourages being happy and making others happy. But it recognizes that

Everything is ultimately a source of suffering because everything is illusion.

happiness is not a solution to life's problems, because it is always temporary."

We were too busy trying to absorb this to ask questions.

"The Second Noble Truth is the solution to suffering. In a nutshell, the solution is to realize that everything is illusion and that suffering comes from the desires produced by illusion. If you free yourself from the illusion, you will no longer suffer.

"That leads to the Third Noble Truth, the fact of nirvana. Nirvana is the state in which there is no illusion, no constant change, and therefore no suffering. It's the state of total, permanent bliss, because there is no desire. After Buddha left this world, he reached nirvana and was reincarnated no more.

THE FOUR NOBLE TRUTHS OF BUDDHISM

1. Existence is *suffering* and illusion.

2. *Suffering* is caused by earthly *desires,* which deny Truth #1.

3. It is possible to escape earthly *desires* in *nirvana.*

4. To realize *nirvana,* one must follow the Eightfold Path.

"The Fourth Noble Truth is the most complicated, because it is how to reach nirvana. We call it the Eightfold Path because it has eight steps. They are all 'right' things: right understanding, right thinking, right speech, right action, right livelihood, right effort, right mindfulness, and right concentration. These apply both to daily life and to the spiritual life, and they lead, ultimately, to nirvana.

"Next, I should describe what Buddhist society is like. Let me be really clear that an ideal Buddhist society in America wouldn't look just like an ideal Buddhist society in Burma, or Japan, or wherever. It would be different in different countries. Besides, there is no ideal Buddhist society. My point is, Buddhism leads to a better society, but not necessarily an *Asian* society.

"Now, about Buddhist society: Buddhism divides people into the holy order and the normal order. The holy order is made up of men and women devoted to a special holy life. We might call them monks and nuns after the Christian tradition. The holy order is called the *sangha,* or community, after the first small group of the Buddha's followers. The sangha live chaste lives, focusing on prayer and meditation.

"Everybody else just lives ordinary lives, raising families and working. Buddhists seek peace and harmony with everything. They don't hurt anything or anybody.

"Buddhism didn't spread by force, and it didn't provoke any great persecutions or cause any sudden societal upheavals. Peacefully and patiently, on their own merit, the Buddha's teachings won over a large number of followers. One convert was the emperor Asoka, a Magadhan emperor in the third century before the Christian era. He ruled most of modern India. Even he didn't force anybody to become Buddhist. On the contrary, Buddhism changed him from a violent warlord into a peace-loving and benevolent leader. He built huge temples all over what's now India and carved inscriptions praising the Buddha and his Path.

"In later centuries, Buddhism split into two major divisions, which eventually divided into lots of smaller branches. Buddhism is so far-flung over East Asia—and beyond!—that it has taken on a wealth of different forms in many locations.

"The two main divisions are called Theravada and Mahayana. Theravada is the more traditional. With Theravada you stick more closely to the records of what Buddha preached and how Buddhists lived in ancient times. It's mostly in Southeast Asia and Sri Lanka. Mahayana is much broader, both in what it practices and how far it has spread. You're more likely to encounter Mahayana today.

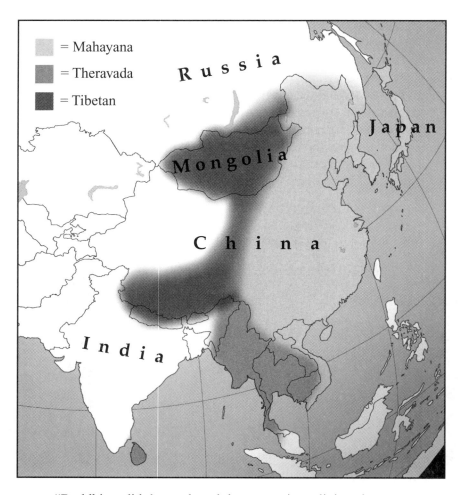

= Mahayana
= Theravada
= Tibetan

Russia

Mongolia

China

Japan

India

   "Buddhism didn't attack and destroy native religions but embraced them and slowly instilled its ethics and morals into them,
bringing a higher level of harmony and civility wherever it reached.
Distinctive forms of Buddhism exist in different countries, like
China, Korea, and Japan. One Japanese form that's gotten popular
lately is Zen Buddhism, which you may have heard of.

   "Ethics are extremely important to Buddhists. Buddhists are
not to harm anyone or to cause suffering in any way. Giving is a
very big part of Buddhist ethics. The sangha are supported completely by donations, or almost completely, I should say. It's also
important to be compassionate to those in need, especially the
sick or injured. Caring for one's family is paramount.

"I guess the last thing I should talk about is meditation. It isn't well understood in the West. People seem to have this idea that meditation is a weird magical act that has you trying to levitate or get better at karate or something. Others think it's a big fraud. But meditation is really a very challenging and fulfilling mental discipline.

"The goal of meditation is to shut down the thinking processes that are instinctive to us in everyday life. Our brains have this innate measuring and categorizing instinct caused by the illusion of the world. We're always trying to analyze and divide things, when in fact, everything is a mirage. In order to gain insight into the way things really are, we have to learn to shut off the thinking process. That is what meditation does."

This was a load of information. Most of it sounded pretty good to me, but Brad had a smart question. "Hey, if you were to boil it all down, what would be the main reason you would give me for becoming Buddhist instead of anything else?"

"I'd say that Buddhism gives you the best of all worlds. It is dedicated to everything peaceful, pure, and loving. Buddhism is orderly to the mind and body. It gives deep fulfillment to the soul and relieves you of pain, worry, and stress. You have security about the future and a guarantee that it is possible to achieve total and eternal bliss. At the same time, it isn't meaningless or empty because you have to work and sacrifice faithfully in order to grow and progress.

"Anything worthwhile in any religion can be found in Buddhism. I would call it the cream of human religion. Whatever kind of person you are, Buddhism offers a way of piety and righteousness. If you're the kind who likes ceremony and devotion, you have plenty of it. If you like cerebral, private experiences, you fit perfectly into Buddhism. If corporate, societal improvement is your burden, you won't find a more congenial and encouraging religion than Buddhism. And I believe the reason Buddhism offers so much is that it is the perfect expression of religion."

Statues of Buddha are a common sight in China and other predominately Buddhist countries.

Can We Deny Everything?

4

Memory Verses: Daniel 12:2–3

"I know a lot of things about them sound alike, but I think there are some serious differences between Hinduism and Buddhism. For one, Hinduism doesn't have an individual founder, but Buddhism does. For another thing, Hindus often live ascetically, but Buddhism teaches the Middle Path—since Gautama gave up on asceticism." Guide Girl was thinking out loud to Brad and me while everyone took yet another break and got ready for Li's cross-examination.

"Yeah. And Buddhists never had anything like the caste system. Remember when Ravi was on the hot seat?"

"But remember, Brad, that Buddha was supposedly a great king in past lives because he had amassed so much good karma. That means you do move up and down in your human lives, even if Buddhists aren't divided into castes like Hindus."

"This stuff just blows my mind," I threw in. "According to both of these guys, I have lived a load of past lives and now I'm living with karma from them, even though I don't remember them. When I die, I'll go who knows where and be who knows what based on how good I've been in this life. The only way to stop being reincarnated is to realize that all of this is true— even though realizing is somehow more than just knowing it."

Brad responded, "That is a strong motive to live right. Buddhism seems to have a lot going for it. What do you think?" he asked Guide.

"I think you boys should be concerned with what is *true,* not what has a lot going for it. If Buddhism is true, then you ought to give dedicated effort to learning about it. But if it's a question of what a religion has going for it, you might as well make up your own, since you are assuming that your own preferences determine what makes a good religion."

"How can we possibly know which religion is 'true'? What has anybody got to go on other than his own preferences?" Brad was a little hot, and Guide's eyes flashed, and I thought a good fight was coming, but just then Ted called us back to the table.

I had to choose who asked questions in what order again. Brad wanted me to start with Ravi so we could hear how he saw the difference between Buddhism and Hinduism.

"I suspect my friend Li knows what question I will ask as well as I do," Ravi began. "I will of course draw our attention to the oldest quandary of Buddhists, the individuality of the soul. Need I even frame the question aloud?"

"Yes!" Brad and I blurted together.

Ravi laughed. "Of course, I will. Gautama accepted most of the tenets held by all Hindus, as Li has pointed out: karma, reincarnation, the illusory nature of the physical world, and the need to escape them all in order to escape suffering and death. However, Gautama taught that there is no individual existence of the soul. Is that not true?"

"Sure, it is," Li answered, like he knew where this was going.

"And yet, you believe that individuals pass from one life to the next enduring or enjoying the result of karma from the preceding lives. Furthermore, you believe that upon entrance to nirvana, Gautama passed from existence—but he did not exist already, if what he taught were true. How do you explain such a contradiction?

"Hindus believe in the principle of karma," Ravi continued, "but we agree that each person is real, a spark from the fire of Brahman that is yet the same fire and will be merged with it again. Yet you followers of Gautama must say that all personality, even thought, is part of the illusion destroyed in nirvana. But to reach nirvana requires much growth and advancement over many lives; Gautama even claimed to have lived thousands of times before. How can the same soul pass through different lives, fulfilling its own karma, when it does not exist?"

How can the same soul pass through different lives, fulfilling its own karma, when it does not exist?

Li nodded and glanced away from Ravi's benign *I've got you* smile. "Yeah, that's the old standby for beating on Buddhism. And like you know, there are a lot of different answers to choose from. The problem is that we're in an area that's hard to understand and talk about with the vocabulary and concepts we are used to. The instinct to always measure and categorize everything intrudes on our ability to grasp sublime, spiritual truths.

"My answer is that the solution lies in your own Hindu beliefs, Ravi, my man. Distinguishing the individual from the whole is an artificial concept. There is no *me* and *you* separate from the *we* or the *One*. You believe that, and that is the answer to your question, whatever else differs about our faiths. You and I and everyone are karmic threads in the infinite tapestry of the universe. It's not so much the result of what I did in past lives that follows me, as you well know, but the karmic essence of what I *am* that follows." (As my big brother Phil used to say, "If you can't convince 'em, confuse 'em.")

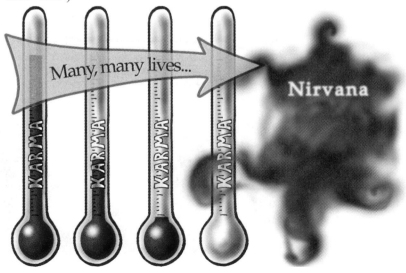

"Enlightenment is not really becoming a superior being but realizing the truth. It means actually knowing, *experiencing,* that we are not separate entities but all branches of one entity. I can't explain further, and neither can you. I'm not a Buddha. But it doesn't seem to me to be a very strong argument that if the soul isn't an independent being, there can be no karma, no reincarnation, and no nirvana. On the contrary, I think the nonexistence of the soul is not only consistent with but foundational to Buddhism."

I noticed Ted nearly coming out of his seat, and since I didn't understand enough of what Li had said to question him, I told Ted to go ahead. "Yeah," he started, "nirvana and stuff aside, I have a problem with Buddhists in this world. Buddhists are notorious for wasting huge amounts of resources on temples, shrines, and ceremonies of devotion. Spending fortunes on those things supposedly improves one's karma. At the same time you have working people giving so much for the sake of karma, you stifle their ability to produce the things they need to live—things you call illusion! What's worse, you have this enormous number of people living as monks or nuns, dependent on charity. They elicit their charity from ordinary people by promising that it will improve karma, or eliminate karma, however you say it. Aren't these people little more than parasites?"

Ouch. Li took a long breath and said, "OK. It sounds like you are going after the way Buddhists spend their money. That's a fair question; a person's

money goes where his values are. I'll try to explain the Buddhist understanding of wealth.

"The world around us and everything in it is an illusion, but that doesn't mean it's irrelevant. Because we are so caught up in it, we are all affected by it. Part of the process of reaching above the world is to use it in such a way that you alter the effect it has on you. Normally, the world aggravates your passions. But you can use the world in such a way that it actually helps you to see that it is all an illusion. Seeing it as an illusion moves you closer to enlightenment.

"To use material things in a way that shows you what they really are, you have to do what is contrary to normal desires. That means giving money away instead of hoarding it or buying things for yourself with it. Charity not only benefits the poor; it also improves the giver.

"That is the reason Buddhists give money to build temples. Temples aren't used to amass wealth or power or fame for the builder. Instead, they serve the spiritual good of the community by giving everyone a place to focus on transcendent spiritual things. Building temples and shrines is a high form of charity.

"As for the sangha, they voluntarily give up many pleasures and comforts. It's not like being a monk is an easy life! Living off charity normally means living at the poverty line. They do without money, families of their own, and most modern conveniences. At the same time, they do a lot for other people, like taking care of orphans and educating children for free. I don't think I would call them parasites."

Li looked unhappy. Ted rolled his eyes around at me like he thought Li was nuts. I looked at Brad.

"I think I'd like to know the purpose for the sangha," Brad said. "Are they people who are farther along the road to enlightenment?"

"I would say usually, but not necessarily. They are people who focus their efforts more on attaining enlightenment than a layperson can."

"Are they reincarnated as monks after not being monks in an earlier life?"

"Well, they certainly weren't monks or nuns in all of their previous lives. Becoming a monk is something you choose. Most often, people in the sangha care more about improving themselves spiritually, but that doesn't mean they are good to begin with. Sometimes a really bad person becomes a monk in order to rid himself of harmful karma through concentrated study and meditation."

Guide Girl asked, "Why would someone *not* want to be a monk? Are laypersons considered spiritually inferior to monks and nuns? I mean, aren't you saying that laypersons are less interested in spiritual advancement—and therefore less likely to advance toward enlightenment—than the sangha, or else they would choose to be part of the sangha?"

"Obviously someone has to feed the sangha, or else they couldn't spend all that time meditating," Li responded. "Hey, I'm not a monk. I've taken some time off to stay at the temple and just read and meditate, like a week or so. But I'm not a member of the sangha. Anyone can advance toward enlightenment."

"Can your gurus, your authoritative teachers, be laypersons?" Guide continued.

"No, I don't think so. At least I've never met a guru who wasn't part of the sangha."

"So it is fortunate that not every Buddhist is excessively interested in reaching enlightenment, or there would be no one to feed and house those who teach you how to reach enlightenment?"

Li shifted in his seat. "I wouldn't say that. Like I said, you don't have to be a monk or nun to advance toward enlightenment. The sangha serves a purpose for the whole community. Everyone is better off because of them; they do good for people other than themselves."

Guide Girl was done, so I had to pick the next questioner. Jack had been so brief last time; I decided to save him for last. "Hey Carla! Go ahead." She didn't need any more prodding.

"Gladly! All right, Li, here's what I want to know: How can the Buddha have discovered the knowledge necessary for enlightenment if progress toward enlightenment requires the suppression of critical thinking and the abandonment of an investigative attitude?

"I realize that many people find peace and contentment in Buddhism. I think that's wonderful. I wouldn't take that away from anybody. But if you want to persuade the rest of us to take up Buddhism for ourselves, you have to answer some serious objections. That's why I want to know how you can even claim knowledge or justify communicating through language when you think nirvana is the *absence* of knowledge and thought. I don't see how, even if Buddhism *were* true for me, I could ever depend on learning it from *you*—or anyone else; nothing personal."

So it is fortunate that not every Buddhist is excessively interested in reaching enlightenment?

I decided then that I liked Carla, but I wouldn't want to get into an argument with her. She thought fast and talked fast, and despite her smile you could tell she was looking for a chance to stab you. Li must have thought the same thing, because he took a few seconds to answer.

"Obviously, we all live in the real world. We have to learn in the language and culture of the world, even if it is illusion. It makes sense, at least to me, that if the world we see is all false, but we are completely convinced that it is real, we must first learn about transcendent truth before knowing how to escape it."

That didn't satisfy Brad. "If we are all stuck in the illusion that everything is real, when really nothing is real, then how did we get in this mess to begin with? You say we have all these lives to go through, and that we can do good or bad in them, but the fact that we have them at all is the truly bad thing because we want to escape from life. But how did this get started in the first place?"

"The Buddha never tried to explain the origin of illusion," was Li's quick answer. "He would have considered your question unanswerable, meaning either it doesn't have an answer or that we cannot comprehend the answer until we reach enlightenment. Buddha used the simile of a man shot by an arrow who demands the identity of the person who shot him and a detailed description of the arrow before letting the surgeon save his life. Some questions don't have answers, at least not answers we can understand."

"Are there other questions like that?" I wondered.

"Yeah—but you are supposed to ask questions, not me!" Li laughed. "You can't trick me into questioning myself!"

I didn't know what to do, and Brad only shrugged. All we had left was Jack's question, anyway. My thinker was tired. Another break sounded good. I told Jack he could ask his question.

That deep, rumbly voice again. "Perhaps Li is thinking of the question of what becomes of one who enters nirvana—Does he exist or not? Does he both exist and not exist? Does he neither exist nor not exist?—for that was in the Buddha's view an unworthy question. But it is not my question; I have another."

"Hey, that's not fair!" Li blurted. "You're just supposed to ask a single question during this phase, not give them ideas for more questions."

"I am merely commenting on a point you yourself raised, and supplying information our Quester requested. Furthermore, I am leading into my own question by focusing our attention upon the Buddha.

"To contrast Christianity with Buddhism is to contrast the Christ with the Buddha. Whatever may be built in the name of either faith rests ultimately upon its founder. Therefore I wish to ask a question by which Li can help us to see the difference.

"What—not just who, but *what*—was Siddhartha Gautama, the Buddha? Of course, I expect you to use his own claims as they have been preserved for us, claims I do not challenge. Based on the teachings of Buddhism, I ask you to define for us, as precisely as possible, what the Buddha was."

"OK, but you don't get to ask any follow-up questions, right? They have to ask the follow-ups?" Li gestured toward us. Jack nodded, but I took it as a personal challenge. Li didn't think we could ask the hard questions!

"What was the Buddha?" Li began. "First, he was a human being. That isn't really necessary to Buddhism, but it's true. Gautama was a man. He was normal in every way. He knew what it was like to wrestle with evil desires and deal with the weaknesses of humanity.

"Second, he was more than human. He had advanced (through previous lives) beyond the knowledge of ordinary people. By steady, focused effort he finally achieved enlightenment. At that point, he was still human, but by transcending the illusion of the world he gained knowledge and power that seem incredible to us. Still, it was what every human could have if we could reach enlightenment.

"Third, he entered nirvana and passed into utter, eternal bliss. At that moment he became something we are not, but beyond that nirvana is indescribable. By reaching nirvana, Buddha has reached the apex of human potential. Whatever he is now is perfection."

I tried to think of a good question. Brad beat me to it.

"Did Buddha start out like us, a long time ago, just as far from enlightenment as we are?"

"Yes, I guess so. Isn't that encouraging? Anyone can reach enlightenment just like Gautama did."

Anyone can reach enlightenment just like Gautama did.

"Then what sets Gautama apart?" Guide Girl asked. "There have been so many people throughout history who claimed to have discovered the truth. How did Gautama become the one to find truth instead of someone else? What made him special?"

"He earned it over many incarnations. If you want evidence, I point to the many people who have found his teachings true and satisfying. I think his system leads to greater peace and a better explanation for the way life is than any other religion offers."

Well, I had to ask the question Jack suggested. "So what became of Gautama when he died? He said he would enter nirvana, but exactly what did that do to him? If I'm supposed to work toward the same thing, I'd like to know."

Li rolled his eyes. "Jack knows that that was another question the Buddha wouldn't answer. Knowing what it's like doesn't help you get there, the Buddha said."

"Did Buddha send any messages back from nirvana?" was Brad's last question.

"Of course not!" Li answered. We waited for him to say more, but he didn't.

"Well, let's see." Ted ended the uncomfortable pause with some needed cheerfulness. "We've already had a cake break. How about a coffee break?"

"You know," Brad started, "it seems like all my friends drink coffee, but I've just never gotten around to trying it."

"Me neither," I added.

"There's no better place to start than my favorite, Colombian Revenge!"

Believe me, it lived up to its name. After the first sip, I felt like my taste buds were being attacked by thousands of angry Colombian coffee growers. "Ted," I gasped, "I hope your taste in ideas is better than your taste in coffee."

"Does this mean I'm next?"

"I guess so," Brad said. "The Quester has spoken. Take the hot seat for a while, Ted."

"Well, I am certainly glad to do so. I'm sure that you all have noticed that I have done quite well in this debate. But as I begin my own presentation, let me make something very clear: my strong performance in this debate is not due primarily to my intelligence. The secret to my success is my education. It has taught me that in the search for truth, we must not begin with God or the supernatural. Science has not been able to prove that either exists. Therefore, those who place God and religion at the center of their philosophy inevitably end up constructing a world-view of feelings and hopes that has no basis in fact.

"We must begin with what we know—*that we are human beings and that our greatest power is the power of reason.* Our most important responsibility, therefore, is not to some invisible, unknowable deity. We should concern ourselves with things human, not things divine. Our goal in life must be to preserve and better the human condition. It is irresponsible to assume that the answer to life's troubles is something supernatural, something that cannot even be proved to exist. We cannot trust 'divine guidance' in our search for truth. We must use the only thing that history has proved to be reliable—our capacity for reason empowered by the conclusions of science."

History has never been my best subject, but even I could tell that something was wrong here. It seemed that Ted's claim about history proving his view was pretty vague. Just as I was starting to put a question together in my mind, Brad jumped in.

"OK, let's work on what you've said for a little bit here. If history proves that reason rather than religion is to be trusted, why is it that most people through history have been religious? There have been very few atheistic cultures in the world, and those that have tried to get along without religion haven't done very well. The Communist regimes of the twentieth century were that way. Would you consider those to be a good example of reason being better than religion?"

Yep. Brad was right. Ted was in the hot seat now.

"Of course not," Ted answered. "But there is much more to being a secular humanist than simply rejecting traditional religion."

"So you would consider yourself a secular humanist?" I asked.

"Yes, I am a humanist, and I consider humanism to be the best philosophy of life. Anyway, back to my point. A true humanist has a very optimistic view of human progress and achievement. I believe that man's continual progress is woven into the fabric of the universe. It is in our nature to get better and better. Therefore, unlike the Communists of the last century, I am an ardent proponent of liberty. If people are free, they will progress away from the darkness of superstition and theism toward the light of self-sufficiency and humanism.

"Now concerning your other question, Brad, it is true that most people throughout history have been theists of one sort or another. But it is also true that there have been many humanists throughout history. Humanism is, in fact, quite ancient."

"Older than Christianity?" I asked.

"Yes, much older. It has its roots in classical China and India. Evidence for this early period is a bit sketchy. We get a clearer picture from ancient Greece. The first Greek philosophers that we know of lived during the 500s B.C. They distinguished themselves from earlier thinkers by denying that divine beings—or anything supernatural—produced the natural world. Loosing themselves from the shackles of religion and superstition, they sought a natural explanation for all that happens in nature. These brave pioneers, who were not afraid to ask hard questions, laid the foundation for real progress in philosophy and science. Had the progress resulting from their efforts not been interrupted for over a millennium, there is no telling how advanced our culture would be today."

At this point Ted paused and looked at each of us, no doubt waiting for someone to ask the obvious question. Brad obliged.

"OK, Ted. Who was the 'bogeyman' that messed up humanism for a thousand years?"

"The Christian religion," he said deliberately. "Christianity swept the Roman Empire during the third and fourth centuries A.D.

This new religion taught that humans were basically sinful. Because their minds were twisted by depravity, they could not understand their world through the powers of reason. Humans could come to the truth only by placing unquestioning faith in Jesus Christ and the books of the Old and New Testaments (books supposedly written by God). The teachings of the Greek philosophers, which had been a cornerstone of Roman civilization, came to be viewed as the musings of benighted 'pagans.' But even the obscurantist Christians could not completely deny the merits of these early humanists. Many of the teachings of Plato and Aristotle survived throughout the Christian era. However, they were not used or studied for their own sake. Real philosophical inquiry came to a halt. The works of the Greeks were employed only as an aid to developing Christian theology and religious thought.

"The Christian system of faith destroyed people's confidence in their ability to solve their own problems. It achieved this erosion of confidence through a tyranny of the mind. Early Christians taught that all of human history was the conflict of God's kingdom

Augustine of Hippo (354–430) was one of the outstanding figures of the early Christian church. Although he confined most of his ministry to the city of Hippo, located in North Africa, he proved to be a very influential thinker in the history of Western philosophy. In his most famous work, *The City of God*, he argued that all human history is the story of two cities representing opposing ways of life. One is the city of earth, the home of sinful, unsaved men. The other is the city of God, namely His church. God's purpose in history is to build His city by saving men from sin. These two cities exist side by side in this life but will be separated by God at the final judgment. The earthly city and its citizens will go to the destruction reserved for sinners. Citizens of the heavenly city will go to eternal glory and bliss with God. The effect of this work was to focus Christians on the next life and to lead them to be more concerned with the triumph of the spiritual and eternal than the triumph of the physical and temporal.

St. Augustine *by Gaspar de Craeyer. From the Bob Jones University Collection.*

and the world's kingdom. Though often troubled and disappointed, the true members of God's kingdom would ultimately triumph, living forever with God in the next life. Those of the world, however, no matter how successful they might be in this life, would suffer eternal punishment.

"This teaching concerning the afterlife had a profound effect on Europe, which comprised much of what had been the Roman Empire after the fall of Rome. The hope of an eternity of bliss led many to a lax attitude toward the human condition. Since the 'here and now' is fleeting and therefore unimportant, the problems of human suffering and injustice were viewed as necessary evils that one should simply endure while anticipating the 'sweet by and by.' The effect that this thinking had on science, technology, and education was devastating. Scientific advancement came to a standstill for a thousand years. And during this time illiteracy soared while superstition reigned.

"I should also mention that the fear of 'burning in hell forever' had a damaging effect on social and political life. People were afraid to question authority—particularly religious authority—because they thought they might go to hell for it. Consequently, religion tyrannically dominated every aspect of human affairs. Churchmen controlled education, artistic expression, and government. At points certain popes, who lived in Italy, were able to tell kings living in England and Germany how to govern their lands. For roughly a thousand years (A.D. 500–1500), the glorious light of Greece and Rome was lost. Those ten centuries are appropriately labeled the 'Dark Ages'—a time when Europe wandered in the ignorance and superstition that always result from religious tyranny."

"Well," I broke in. "It's hard to imagine the pope telling the president of the United States what to do. So what happened? Obviously those days are over."

"I'm sure you all have heard of the Renaissance," Ted began. "That term comes from a French word meaning 'rebirth,' and it refers to the period of time from 1300 to 1600. During this time two factors combined to help bring the dark period to an end. First, medieval Europeans were exposed to something better. Throughout the Middle Ages the works of the ancient Greeks and Romans were studied, as I mentioned earlier. But around 1300 they began to be studied for their own sake. As people gained an appreciation for the culture and intellectual achievements of the 'pagans,' they began to question their authoritarian religion. Belief in man as the measure of all things was at that time 'reborn,' if you will.

"Second, religion discredited itself. Churchmen claimed to be servants of God and shepherds of His people. But very often they were caught in scandals exposing them as selfish power-grubbers. People all over Europe began doubting the wisdom of letting their lives be dominated by teachings that could never be proved."

"So that explains how we got here?" Brad asked.

"No, that explains how we started to get here. From 1600 to 1800 an intellectual movement called the Enlightenment grew and flourished. This led Europe out of the ignorance and superstition of the Dark Ages by reasserting confidence in humanity's ability to solve its own problems. One of the earliest proponents of this new view was René Descartes. He taught that reason was the chief source of knowledge for humans and that it therefore had an incredible potential for unveiling how the universe worked. Reason came to replace religion as man's only reliable path to true understanding. So, in contrast to the preceding ten centuries, these two centuries became known as the Age of Reason."

"Oh, so *reason* is the reason that the Age of Reason is called the Age of Reason." You may have guessed it was Brad who said that. Ted continued as though there had been no interruption.

"During this period science and the scientific method were taken as the chief support for this newfound respect for reason. Francis Bacon emphasized the importance of basing knowledge on experimentation and not on prejudice or tradition. The power of such scientific thinking was demonstrated by the labors of Copernicus, Kepler, Galileo, and Newton. Through reason and careful observation they successfully challenged traditional religious superstitions regarding the movement of planets and other heavenly bodies. Religion tried to stifle this growth of knowledge, but once mankind gets a taste of the truth, it is very difficult to convince him that he'd rather have error.

"What emerged from this period of remarkable discovery was a radically different understanding of the universe. Humans learned that the natural world was not controlled by some deity. It was an elaborate machine governed by unalterable laws.

Galileo Galilei (1564–1642) applied the telescope to astronomy to discover topography on the moon, as well as moons around Jupiter.

"This realization had a profound effect on the human condition. Over the past two centuries since the Age of Reason, knowledge and technology have exploded. Humans have conquered their environment and have been able to significantly reduce poverty, disease, and suffering. They have lengthened life expectancy and have vastly improved transportation and communication. By shaking itself free from the bondage of faith, the human race has begun to discover the potential that reason empowered by science has for making the here-and-now a better place."

"So you don't think there's a God?" I asked.

"I don't think there's any credible evidence for believing in a Supreme Being who created the universe."

"Then where did the universe come from?"

"It's always been."

"It's always been what?" asked Brad.

"It's always been in existence. It hasn't always existed in its present form, of course. But since nothing can come from nothing, we must conclude that matter is eternal. And since there is no evidence for the existence of God, we must conclude that its present form is not the result of divine activity but is rather the result of a continuous process of change—evolution, in other words."

"Why do you think there's no evidence for God?" I began. "I mean, it seems to me that there's evidence for Him everywhere. Just look at—"

"What evidence are you talking about? Have you ever seen God—I mean with your physical eyes? Have those two hands actually touched His face?"

"Well, no. But I see the effects of His working all over the place. The orderliness of the world—from the orbiting of the moon to the regular rhythms of my own heart—this is a universe that seems carefully planned and *made*. Not something that just *happened*. Things that just happen don't have this kind of order." I was very proud of myself at this point. I guess my Colombian Revenge had finally started to kick in.

"Have you ever seen a magic show?" Ted asked.

"I think I'm looking at one right now." Brad, of course.

"Well, at a magic show you see things you can't explain. People seem to get cut in half, but they end up being perfectly healthy. Large objects float above the stage. And somehow the magician's little helpers vanish before your very eyes. A small child looks at that and thinks, 'Wow, it's magic!' A mature adult, however, thinks, 'Hmm. I wonder how he did that?' This is the difference between the theist and the humanist. The theist looks at the marvels of our world and concludes that there must be some unseen, mystical reality (that is, God) making these marvels happen—magic, so to speak. The humanist, however, is mature and skeptical. He's seen enough of the world to know that what seems mysterious at first is in fact the operation of the laws of nature. Every time we investigate some marvel of nature, we discover that it's not the hand of God. It's the operation of predictable, explainable natural laws."

"So there's no God and therefore no divine book for us to guide our lives by," Brad said thoughtfully. "How do we determine what's right and wrong?"

"The only reliable path to knowledge is human reason informed by science. I come to know things through the correct use of my intellect based on the unprejudiced conclusions of scientific experimentation."

"But how do scientific experiments teach a person how to live?" Brad asked.

"Experimentation alone doesn't. We must use reason—careful thinking that follows the accepted rules of logic—together with science. To those who are accustomed to looking to some external authority for moral direction, this may seem strange. I, however, believe in the dignity and self-sufficiency of man. Humans are rational beings who possess within themselves the ability to ascertain truth and morality. I don't see how a thinking person can come to any other conclusion. Science tells us that we cannot look to 'God' for guidance, and experience teaches us that humans are the most intellectually advanced beings on the planet. To look outside of ourselves—or to ignore our powers of reason—is irresponsible. No deity will save us; we must save ourselves."

"Save ourselves from what?" Brad asked.

"Save ourselves from all that plagues the human condition—war, disease, poverty, crime, and deterioration of the environment. These are the woes that impede the progress of the human race, and these are the enemies that every humanist is committed to defeating."

"What about hell? How do we save ourselves from hell?" I asked.

"Reason informed by science offers no credible evidence that humans survive the death of their bodies. Therefore, I believe that talk of heaven and hell is misguided and harmful.

The enemies of human advancement

It distracts people from working to save themselves from the things they do know and understand—like disease and poverty."

"Ted, I don't think you've answered my question," Brad interrupted. "I'm still not clear on how you can tell the difference between right and wrong."

"Since science and reason tell me nothing about a metaphysical world, I must conclude that it cannot be known and therefore either does not exist or is not relevant for us. The goal of life, which is foundational for ethics, must thus be concerned with the here and now. I believe that we all exist to serve mankind's greatest good in the here and now. Ethical conduct should be judged by human reason, based on an understanding of what makes humans happy and leads to social justice."

"So being happy and having justice are the things that tell you what's right and what's wrong?" Brad.

"Yes, I'd agree with that assessment."

"But it seems to me that the two would always be at odds. Whenever justice is served, someone is unhappy, right? I mean, on TV, whenever the judge bangs his gavel, somebody is really mad."

"Well, Brad, it's not as difficult as you're trying to make it sound. The basic principles of morality are universal. All civilizations—whether religious or humanistic—have basically the same understanding of right and wrong, and all civilizations have a similar understanding of what makes people happy. As we all have evolved throughout the millennia of our existence, these moral and aesthetic tendencies have evolved with us. The classic expression of the ideal of human morality is the Golden Rule: 'Do to others what you would want them to do to you.' Or I could state it negatively: 'Don't treat other people in a way that you would not want to be treated.'"

"Hmm. That sounds familiar," I muttered.

"Now, I will grant that occasionally some humans will insist that in their pursuit of happiness they must do something that others believe is unjust. In such circumstances it would seem that happiness and justice conflict. But we do not have to appeal to some religious, metaphysical authority to resolve this conflict. I think this conflict should be resolved by appealing to the objective use of reason based on the Golden Rule.

"For example, suppose a dispute involves two men named George and Bill. To solve the problem, we should objectively ask ourselves whether Bill's happiness involves treating George in a way that any reasonable person would not want to be treated. If so, justice is served by blocking Bill's pursuit of happiness. This act does deny one person's pursuit of happiness, but it preserves the happiness of society in general, because no one would feel safe or satisfied in a society where people are allowed to abuse others for their own satisfaction. Furthermore, this action has the potential of making even Bill happy: it teaches him the importance of valuing the rights of other people. And as we all know, no man can be truly happy as long as he is hurting others.

"So, Brad, what results in all of this is an ethical system that has a strong commitment to freedom but that limits freedom when it threatens the freedom or happiness of others. Since I would prefer to be able to make my own choices without being condemned or coerced, I allow others to enjoy freedom of choice. But since I would not want someone to use his freedom to harm me, I insist that freedom of choice be limited so that no one is allowed to make choices that harm other people."

"If you're so concerned about freedom," Carla broke in, "why is so much of the humanist agenda aimed at denying people their freedoms?"

"Whoa, Carla!" I couldn't believe she was ignoring the rules. "You can't ask questions right now. This is supposed to be—"

"What are you referring to?" Ted asked.

"The whole 'separation of church and state' thing—especially as it concerns education. I think parents ought to be able to send their children to religiously based schools if they want to."

Well, it sounded interesting, so I just thought I'd let them go at it. Besides, at this point it was clear to me that I had pretty much become invisible.

"In the United States they can."

"Not without spending a ton of money on top of their taxes, which are supposed to pay for their kids' education. Ted, it seems to me that a freedom-loving philosophy would allow for religious expression in the public school classroom and in the meetings of our government. It also would not oppose distributing government funds to religious institutions that truly benefit society as a whole."

"Carla, you have to understand that humanism is characterized by two pervasive attitudes: secularism and tolerance. I am a secularist; that is, I believe that public life (government and education primarily) should be kept free from religious expression. As a humanist, however, I am also tolerant. I believe that people should be free to think what they wish and that they should be free to express it. To be intolerant of others' views—religious or otherwise—is to be inhumane."

"That's my point. Your secularism seems to rule out your tolerance."

"No, no, Carla. The opposite is true. My secularism makes true tolerance possible. By insisting that religion be kept out of civil affairs and education, I preserve freedom. We dare not ignore what history has taught us—when one religion gets special favor in the public square, opposing viewpoints are threatened. By insisting that religion stay out of government and education, I do call for a limitation of religious people's liberties. But if those liberties are not thus limited, the whole idea of liberty will soon be jeopardized."

At this point Li spoke up—might as well, right? "Ted, I think we should try going in a different direction for a while. Several times in this discussion, you have mentioned the importance of improving the human condition in the here and now. How does a humanist plan to go about doing that—in particular?"

At this point I decided there was no sense in trying to make everyone stick to the rules that Guide told me about. From here on I just tried to keep up.

"The secular humanist has three key methods for bettering the human condition. The first is the scientific method."

That's when I decided to remind everyone that I still existed: "You know, I've heard a lot about the scientific method in school and stuff, but I'm not really sure what it refers to."

"Have you ever done a science-fair project?"

"Oh, please don't bring that up, Ted," Brad moaned. "Last year I had the grand idea of feeding coffee grounds to mice—you know, to prove that caffeine is bad for you. How boring! All they did was act a little weird. At the fair, when everybody else had some small furry dead thing to show off, I just had normal mice."

"Well, then, you have personal experience with the scientific method. It's simply a systematic procedure for investigating the world around us. The particulars of the scientific method vary, depending on what is being investigated—whether it's the life cycle of certain insects, the growth of cancerous tumors, the orbiting of a comet, or in your case, the effects of caffeine on mice. Generally it involves observing phenomena, formulating a hypothesis based on that observation, experimenting according to certain accepted rules, and stating a conclusion that validates or modifies the hypothesis. Sometimes the scientist's conclusion becomes the basis for a systematic scheme, or a scientific theory. These theories are educated guesses that help us predict the future and give guidance for other observations and experiments."

"Like the theory of evolution?" I asked.

"Right. The theory of evolution is based on a number of carefully documented observations of nature. From those observations scientists have inferred a general explanation that attempts to explain all of these observations."

"And why is this scientific method important for the humanist?" Brad asked.

"Because it is the best method known to man for understanding this world. When I notice that a number of five-year-olds in American public schools are having difficulty learning and behaving well, my first reaction is not to open the Bible and see what it says about kids and their behavior. To me, that is tragically irresponsible. I employ the scientific method—I do an experiment, in other words. If you doubt the superiority of this approach to solving problems and learning more about the world, just look at history. The use of the scientific method has an impressive track record. In the last two centuries, it has been used systematically and extensively. And the results have been astounding. We understand our world better now than we ever have. In fact, we have—"

"Yeah, I know, I know. The Dark Ages, the Age of Reason, and the dread curse of Christianity," Brad said. "What about your second key method for improving the human condition?"

"Free inquiry is also of vital importance. By this I mean freedom of the press, freedom of speech, freedom to organize opposition parties, and freedom to conduct and publish scientific research of all kinds. Citizens should be allowed to freely voice their criticisms of political leaders. Scientists should be free to conduct experiments and studies without being stopped for supposedly 'moral' reasons. Schools ought to be places that invite students to question traditional authority so that they can learn for themselves what they believe. No teacher should be forced to teach under a 'gag order.' Young people should be encouraged to ask any question—especially the hard ones."

"And why is free inquiry so important?" I asked.

"We must respect the right of individuals to express their beliefs—no matter how unpopular they may be—because we are more likely to discover truth if we can freely exchange opposing views. So by defending and encouraging free inquiry, I unshackle humans to follow their natural course of progress and discovery. This, by the way, is true for every aspect of human endeavor. Not just science, but also religion and morality."

"And your last method?" Brad asked.

"Education. This is the most important method we have for building a more humane, free, and democratic society. Through education the humanist passes on to each new generation the living tradition of human knowledge gained through reason and the use of the scientific method. Thus, education is vital for the progress of the human race. If we fail to pass on to the next generation the things we have learned, the social and intellectual development of our race—which has increased at such an impressive rate over the last two centuries—could come to a tragic halt."

"À la the Dark Ages," Brad said.

"Exactly!"

Secular humanism's three key methods for improving the human condition:

1. The scientific method
2. Free inquiry
3. Education

"And that's the reason," Brad began, "that you oppose government funding for education that is pervasively reli—"

"Yes, of course." Ted cut him off.

"And that's the reason that you oppose the teaching of Creationism in science classrooms?" Brad finished.

"Correct. The theory of evolution has impressive support from many different sciences. Therefore, I strongly oppose the efforts by ignorant Christians to insist that Creationism be taught as science. This threatens academic freedom and the integrity of science as we know it. It is inexcusable to represent as science what is in fact nothing more than an article of religious faith. Such a course of action could derail mankind's scientific progress for generations to come."

"OK, Ted, I think we've got a pretty clear picture of humanism," Brad said. "Carla, what's your take on what Ted is saying?"

The skyscrapers that dominate the skylines of many cities in the West remind the humanist of modern man's triumph over nature, poverty, and ignorance.

Carla thought for a moment and then said, "Well, I guess my biggest problem is Ted's misrepresentation of history."

"What do you mean?" Ted asked.

"You talk as though atheism has rescued humanity from being destroyed by religion."

"I do think humanism has rescued much of the world from the tyranny of religious thought. We still have a long way to go, though."

"See, that's my point. There's this ambitious 'take over' mentality that dominates your worldview. 'We still have a long way to go,' you say, as though you're an army general campaigning against some opposing group of human beings. To me that is itself inhumane. You are out to rob other people of their rights, of their individual identity—of the very things that make them happy."

"Well," Ted began, "you obviously haven't been listening very closely to what I've been saying for the past—"

" 'We dare not ignore what history teaches us.' That's what you said at one point. Now let me rephrase it a bit so that it reflects my thinking: We dare not ignore the fact that history demonstrates humanism is a repressive ideology."

"No, no, Carla. Humanism has freed the race through the advancement of science and technology. We are no longer slaves to our environment, slaves to our superstitions, slaves to—"

"Maybe so. But we have in the process become slaves to our technology. The scientific advancements that you are so proud of have nearly destroyed the human race. The frightening, destructive power of nuclear weapons is the result of technology. So thanks to technology, we have exchanged fear of the bubonic plague for fear of nuclear holocaust. Furthermore, I'm not so sure that life in the Middle Ages was all that bad."

"Oh, c'mon, Carla. Those people lived like animals!"

"And most of us today live like machines. Our labor-saving devices multiply our sense of drudgery. Our amusements bore us. And our time-saving devices rob us of the leisure time we need to think and reflect on life."

"Well, at least we don't have to worry that churchmen are controlling our government and our educational system," Ted fired back.

"That, Ted, is a comfort only if you're a secular humanist. This is the same attitude that fueled the oppressive communistic regimes of the twentieth century. Their concern to 'free' mankind from religion motivated them to violate the human rights of anyone who didn't want to be thus 'free.' "

"Obviously you do not understand what today's secular humanism is all about. I happen to have with me the *Humanist Manifestos I and II.* Under 'Democratic Society' on page 19, Manifesto II states, 'To enhance freedom and dignity the individual must experience a full range of *civil liberties* in all societies. This includes freedom of speech and . . . religious liberty.' That sounds like a pretty strong commitment to freedom of religion, if you ask me."

"Wrenched out of context, yes. Let me see that thing." Ted handed Carla his copy of the *Humanist Manifestos I and II.* "Hmm, let's see . . . here it is," she began. "The thirteenth affirmation of Manifesto I, on pages 9–10, is as follows:

Religious humanism maintains that all associations and institutions exist for the fulfillment of human life. . . . Certainly religious institutions, their ritualistic forms, ecclesiastical methods, and communal activities must be reconstituted as rapidly as experience allows, in order to function effectively in the modern world.

"Whoa!" I said. "Say that in English, Carla."

"In other words, it is the mission of secular humanists to take control of religious institutions and make them humanistic. *That* sounds like a strong commitment to violating human rights—if you ask me."

"OK, it is true that when Manifesto I was published (in 1933), it affirmed Communism. In the decades that followed, however, the weaknesses of that system became obvious. Today, most secular humanists in America reject Communism and its tendency to force progress on people by violating their right to freely practice their religion. This is evidenced in *A Secular Humanist Declaration,* which I also have with me. . . . Yes, here it is in the introduction, on page 7: 'This declaration defends only that form of secular human-ism which is explicitly committed to democracy. It is opposed to all varieties of belief that . . . espouse rule by dictatorship.' "

"So you've changed your mind since 1933 because you real-ized that the old kind of humanism was wrongheaded?"

Mao Zedong (1893–1976), Joseph Stalin (1879–1953), and Vladimir Lenin (1870–1924) have gone down in history as the most influential Communist leaders of the twentieth century. Instructively, they also will be long remembered as three of the world's cruelest dictators. Pursuing the idea that an athe-istic government should control every aspect of national life, each of these men headed repressive regimes that showed little regard for human life. In an attempt to "free" others from the "vileness" of religion and capitalism, these men enslaved millions with the inhu-mane abuse that necessarily resulted from their misguided ideology.

"Yes, Carla, you could say that. Experience has taught us to revise our previous theories. That's one of the strengths of humanism. Since humanists do not live by faith, they are open to changing their positions when the evidence is strong enough."

"Well, that's easy for an American humanist to say, who is part of a largely non-humanistic society. The fact is, however, that the atheistic regimes of the twentieth century were pretty dense when it came to realizing the faults of their own governments. They changed only because they had to. And I don't think it would have been any different in America if secular humanism had been allowed to take over the country in the early 1930s. You would have clutched your power—with all of its abuses—right to the end."

"Of course you realize that you have no way of knowing that," Ted answered.

"Let me see your *Secular Humanist Declaration,*" Carla said. Ted quietly obeyed. "There are several quotations I'm looking for. . . . OK, here's the first, on page 12:

> Secular humanists believe in the principle of the separation of church and state. . . . Clerical authorities should not be permitted to legislate their own parochial views. . . . Nor should tax revenues be exacted for the benefit or support of sectarian religious institutions. Individuals . . . should be free to accept or not to accept any belief . . . without being compelled by taxation to contribute to those religious faiths with which they do not agree."

"Right. That's a fine statement. I'd agree with that," Ted said.

"Well, I'm not done. Here's the next quotation, from pages 16–17:

> We believe that moral development should be cultivated in children and young adults. We do not believe that any particular sect can claim important values as their exclusive property; hence, it is the duty of public education to deal with these values. . . . Although children should learn about the history of religious moral practices, these young minds should not be indoctrinated in a faith."

"Sounds like good advice to me," Ted added.

"Last and certainly not least are this document's comments regarding the mass media, on pages 22–23:

> Television, radio, films, and mass publishing too often cater to the lowest common denominator and have become banal wastelands. . . . Of special concern to secularists is the fact that the media . . . are inordinately dominated by a pro-religious bias. . . . We believe that television directors and producers have an obligation to redress the balance and revise their programming."

"So are you making a point with all of this?" Ted asked.

"I am—trust me. You say that you are committed to free inquiry and tolerance. And yet you insist on limiting the rights of religious people. You excuse these limitations by saying that without them the liberties of everybody else would be endangered. But what I am observing from these three quotations is that secular humanism practices what it seeks to protect society from—religious intolerance. You say that everyone should have the right to express his views, but you also say that religion should have no part in our government or in the education of our children, and that the presence of religious programming on TV and radio must be significantly reduced. How in your world do people enjoy freedom of religion if they are not permitted to express their religious beliefs in government, education, or the mass media?"

"In the world that I envision, religion has its place. It's just that it should not be forced on others."

The Humanist's Vision for Religious Liberty

"And letting religious institutions be tax exempt or letting them buy airtime on radio and TV is forcing religion on others?"

"Religion should not be given special treatment. Religious organizations should bear the burden of taxation like everybody else."

"Everybody but you."

"What do you mean, Carla? I pay taxes. I'm not tax exempt because I'm a humanist."

"Well, of course *you're* not tax exempt. No individual is. But humanism's most important means of promoting itself is—*public education.* It's much more than tax exempt. It's part of the government, which means that it is *funded* by tax dollars. And it clearly favors secular humanism. There's not a word in the *Humanist Manifestos I and II* or in *A Secular Humanist Declaration* that would be unacceptable in the public school classroom. But precious little of a religion's statement of faith would be allowed. So when I read that people should be allowed to live 'without being compelled by taxation to contribute to those religious faiths with which they do not agree,' I am struck by the blatant hypocrisy."

"We're just trying to help society progress away from traditionalism and superstition," Ted said defensively.

"What you're saying is that humanists should not be forced to pay for the propagation of others' views, but non-humanists must be forced to pay for the propagation of humanism. That is hypocritical, and it shows that not much has changed since 1933. You may reject Communism, but you still embrace the essence of its repression. You still subscribe to the gist of that frightening statement . . . uh . . . let's see . . . where is that quote? Yes, here it is: 'Certainly religious institutions . . . must be reconstituted as rapidly as experience allows in order to function effectively in the modern world.'"

"I would never impose my beliefs on a religious institution. That would—"

"No, but you would insist that the government pass laws that keep them from educating our youth, from making use of our mass media, and from writing or enforcing our laws."

"Well, we cannot let ourselves regress into the Dark Ages. We must not forsake the heritage left to us by those who pioneered the scientific revolution of the Enlightenment."

"You know, Ted, that was a problem I had with your historical survey," Jack said. "You represented the Renaissance and the Age of Reason as though they were dominated by atheists. That simply is not true. Copernicus, Kepler, Galileo, Newton, and Descartes were all Christians. And if you read their writings you will discover that their religious faith and desire to please God motivated their endeavors. Atheists didn't deliver us from the Dark Ages. For the most part Christians did."

"Umm, excuse me?" Guide Girl interrupted. "Could we possibly let Ravi or Li have a chance to ask a question?"

"Yeah, Carla," Brad added. "I'd say you've had the floor, *the walls, and the ceiling* for the past ten minutes. How about you, Li? What do you think of Ted's ideas?"

"Buddha taught that the material world is a place of bondage. The more concerned we get with material things, the more bound we become, and the more we open ourselves to hurt. If I spend no time thinking about the spirit world (as is evidently the case with Ted), I become attached to desires that cannot be eternally satisfied. I end up loving people who will die, places that will be destroyed, and things that will decay and fall apart. So my question to you, Ted, is how do you keep your preoccupation with the material

Sir Isaac Newton was one of the most brilliant scientists of the Enlightenment. His *Principia* redefined how astronomers viewed the movement of celestial bodies. Near the end of this very influential work, Newton summarizes his ideas in a way that reveals he was no atheist or agnostic. "This most beautiful system of the Sun, planets and comets, could only proceed from the counsel and dominion of an intelligent and powerful Being. . . . This Being governs all things, not as the soul of the world, but as the Lord of all."

world from harming you? How do you deal with life's disappointments and tragedies?"

"I understand what you're saying, Li," Ted answered, "but I don't see that any of us has a real choice here. You speak of the spirit world, but you are unable to produce any evidence for it. Without evidence I am not going to believe in it. I think it's better to desire things that exist for only a short time than to desire things that don't exist at all."

"How about you, Ravi?" Guide Girl asked.

"My concern is much like Li's. Ted, your worldview gives no attention to life after death. You defend your position by insisting that every thinking person must admit that there is no evidence for life after death. But I see things very differently. To me, any thinking person cannot help but ponder life after death. All of us will die someday, and we will spend much more time beyond this life than in it. Therefore, it seems irresponsible to say that consideration of an afterlife is irrelevant. I believe I have a good basis for being more concerned about the next life than I do about this one. Furthermore, if philosophy is the study of ultimate questions—"

"Hold on," Brad said. "What are 'ultimate questions'?"

Humanism fails to give an answer to one of philosophy's most important questions— "Where am I going?"

"Questions about ultimate reality. The most common are the following three: 'Where did I come from?'; 'Why am I here?'; and 'Where am I going?' It seems that humanism fails to ask a very important ultimate question, the last of these three, 'Where am I going?' What good is a philosophy that refuses to seek an answer to one of the world's most important ultimate questions? Now, Ted, it may be that I am misrepresenting your views. So I shall ask you directly: do you think that this ultimate question is irrelevant?"

"It is true that I refuse to ask that question—yes," Ted answered. "However, to me, that refusal is a mark of intellectual maturity. Since there are no good answers to that question, I refuse to seek one. And this takes me back to Carla's unfair tirade. She says that I'm being hypocritical because I insist that government, education, and the media be dominated by secularists. I do not see this as hypocrisy, because secularists are more objective than religious people. Those who are committed to a religious tradition are committed to wishful thinking. They believe in life after death and in the existence of God not because there's good evidence but just because they want to. Such people should not be in charge of our government or the education of our children, nor should their unsubstantiated beliefs about the world be allowed to saturate television programming."

"What makes you think there is no good evidence for God's existence?" Jack asked.

"As I said before, reason informed by science offers no credible evidence for believing in a Supreme Being who created the universe. Such a statement doesn't mean that I'm stubborn. I'm willing to be convinced of anything—if the evidence is compelling. So, for example, I used to doubt that smoking was bad for a person's health. Now, however, I'm convinced that it is harmful. But it's not because a holy book somewhere said so. Sound reasoning and evidence convinced me. Study after study has demonstrated that there is an impressive positive correlation between tobacco use and various kinds of cancer. I have not yet seen any such evidence indicating that there is a God."

"That is a very simplistic view of knowledge," Jack said.

"How do you figure that?"

"Seeing clear physical evidence is not the only way that we come to know that something exists. It is extremely simplistic to say that you must be able to see or feel something before you can believe in it. Different entities are proved to exist through different means. Many entities that we all believe in cannot be proved in the fashion you just described. The uniformity of nature, laws of morality, laws of logic—these are all things that each of us would defend as real, but none of them can be seen or touched."

"That's not what I'm saying. I simply mean that we should not be convinced by anything that does not make proper use of the laws of logic or does not offer good evidence."

"So logic is very important to you in proving something?" Jack asked.

"Well, obviously. Logic is the only way to prove whether something is true or false," Ted answered.

"Really? My question to you then is, How do you prove that statement itself?"

"Prove what statement?"

" 'The use of logic is the only way to prove something'—that one. How do you prove that statement?"

"Well, I don't think I should have to. The statement is obvious and self-verifying."

"Ted, I don't think you realize the philosophical bind you've just put yourself in. You're on the horns of a dilemma for which your worldview has no good answer."

"Oh, don't be ridiculous. My worldview is the only objective one available. It's the only one that does not depend on circular reasoning. You're a Christian. If you're like most Christians, you will try to argue for the validity of your worldview by asserting that it is taught in the Bible. The argument goes something like this: 'The Bible is the Word of God; therefore, all that it says is true. The Bible teaches that it is the Word of God and that Christianity is the only true religion; therefore, the Bible is the Word of God and Christianity is the only true religion.' This is not based on sound reasoning; it's embarrassingly circular."

"You say," Jack began, "that reason is the only valid way—"

"Neither is your worldview based on solid evidence or valid experimentation," Ted interrupted. "Of course, you'll probably try to say that you have good evidence for what you believe by pointing to the created order, the effect of the Bible on history, the many instances of fulfilled prophecy, and the personal change that the Bible has on the lives of many individuals. But these too depend on circular reasoning. Each requires a supernatural explanation, and this is the key question in the debate between atheists and theists— *does the supernatural really exist?* You cannot argue for your supernaturalistic worldview by appealing to the supernatural. That's circular reasoning. You cannot use what you are trying to prove as a part of your proof."

"You say that reason is the only valid way to examine a statement that claims to be true, right?" Jack began.

"Right. Absolutely," Ted answered.

"Then my question to you is, How do you prove that claim itself? If you claim that reason proves the statement, then you are reasoning in a circle. You are using reason to prove that reason is the only valid way to prove something. If, on the other hand, you claim to be able to prove the statement without the use of logic or reason, then you have effectively refuted the statement. In that case reason would not be the only valid way of proving something."

Christianity's Circular Reasoning

1. What the Bible says is true.

And

2. The Bible claims that it is true.

Therefore

"So you think we should just forget reason. Just be unreasonable and try to—"

"No, not at all," Jack interrupted. "Reason is very important. Without it we would not be able to have this discussion. The laws of logic are real and must be carefully followed or else there can be no meaningful communication. My point is to prove that even you engage in circular reasoning. We all do at points. It is unavoidable. Every worldview begins with a set of presuppositions."

"Presup-uh—what?!" I asked.

"Presuppositions. Things that we assume to be true without being convinced by evidence that they are true. Every worldview begins by believing in a number of things that it does not attempt to prove. Ted dismisses the Christian worldview as indefensible because it presupposes that the Bible is the Word of God. But, of course, I can just as easily dismiss his worldview because he assumes that reason informed by the scientific method is the only reliable path to truth."

"OK, Jack," Ted began, "so it seems that you believe there are other paths to truth. Name one."

"Divine revelation. What God says is to be trusted because God is absolutely true. This revelation is preserved for mankind in the sixty-six books of the Old and New Testaments."

"See! There you go with that circular reasoning. Before you can use the Bible as evidence, you must prove that it is the Word of God."

Humanism's Circular Reasoning

1. Reason is the only way to find the truth.

And

Therefore

2. This statement is reasonable.

"And there you go with *your* circular reasoning. When you say, 'prove that the Bible is the Word of God' you mean, 'use reason aided by the scientific method.' Thus, you assume that this is the only path to truth, and that is your unproven assumption. You see, Ted, you think that your worldview is the only one that is not ultimately founded on faith, but you're wrong. You too have your presuppositions, and therefore you too live by faith."

"I do not live by faith. I live by *evidence!*" By this time Ted was definitely getting hot.

"But your presupposition that reason is the only path to truth defines for you what legitimate evidence is. That amounts to faith. It's not a question of whether you live by faith. You do—we all do. My faith is in the Bible and the God that it reveals. Yours is in reason and science."

"Well, even if what you say is true, all you've done is demonstrate that we both base our views on faith. You haven't demonstrated that your worldview is *better* than mine."

There Is No Foundation

7

Memory Verses: Romans 1:18–21

That's when I decided to step in. "Let's not go there yet, Ted. I think Jack will get his chance to talk in a little while. I want to hear from Carla first. She had some pretty interesting things to say about humanism. I'll bet her view of the world is something worth listening to."

Brad then gave the official invitation: "OK, Carla, you're up to bat."

"Well," she began, "let me start out by setting a historical context for my beliefs. I'd like to give you a brief history of the study of epistemology by focusing on the thinking of a few very influential individuals."

"Episte—what?!" I asked.

"Epistemology. It's one of the most important aspects of any philosophy or worldview. It is the study of the nature, basis, and extent of knowledge. Have you ever wondered, 'What is truth?' or 'How can I know what is real and what is unreal?' or 'Is it possible to know that something is true and it still not be true?' "

"Like how can you know there is a God, or how can you know that a historical event really happened, or—"

"Yes, I think you've got the idea. These are the kinds of questions that epistemology asks. Biology studies the structure, function, and growth of living organisms; epistemology studies knowing. It aims to determine what we can know, how we can know it, and—ultimately—what it means to know something.

> *Epistemology is the study of the nature, basis, and extent of knowledge.*

"To begin with, let me say that I see myself as one who is actively involved in a major epistemological shift in the history of the West—by *West* I mean basically Europe and the United States. This culture's understanding of itself and of epistemology is now in the middle of a radical change. The 'modern era' seems to be coming to a close. It appears the West is now entering a 'postmodern era.' "

"Wait a minute here," I said. "*Modern* means 'right now.' So how can any current movement or school of thought be '*postmodern*'?"

"Of course, the word *modern* can refer to that which is current. But in the history of the West, philosophers and historians have regularly referred to the time period stretching from 1500 to their own present as the 'Modern Age.' But now that the philosophical ideas that have dominated the West from 1500 to the end of the twentieth century are being questioned and rejected by many, it seems only natural (even though it sounds a little weird) to call this new era of thought the 'Postmodern Age.' Anyway, let's start by talking about the time period just before the dawn of modernity—the Middle Ages."

"And this is the part of history you really like, right?" I asked.

"Why would you say that?"

"Well, you spent a lot of time telling Ted that he was wrong for being so negative about this period—you know, the 'Dark Ages' and all that."

"Right, but that doesn't mean I really like this time period. My point with Ted was that it is wrong to think of the Middle Ages as the disease and modernity as the cure. It is indeed tragic that the medieval period was dominated by religious superstition—there's no doubt about that. But the modern period has been dominated by rationalistic superstition—and in my mind there's certainly no doubt about that either."

"But you defended Christianity and the rights of Christians against Ted's attempts to keep religion out of government, education, and the media," I said.

"I was defending the rights of human beings from other human beings who think it is their right to rob people of their rights. Well, we'll get to my religious beliefs in due course. I want to return to my historical survey now.

"Let's see . . . where were we? Oh, I remember: epistemology in the Middle Ages. During this 'premodern' period, the foundation of knowledge was the being and character of God. So if you were to ask a premodern how it was that a person could know something, he would say something like this: *God exists and He knows all things perfectly.* As human beings made in His image and loved by Him, we are able to know things because *this God communicates some of His knowledge to man.* He communicates to man through several different means—nature, the church, the Holy Spirit, history—but chiefly He communicates through the Scriptures. Our finite knowledge is a subset of His infinite knowledge, given to us through the Holy Scriptures. Now, as you can see, all of this is based on the assumption that an infinite, all-knowing God exists.

Premodern Epistemology

"Well, as has already been suggested, one of the things that bridges the premodern and modern periods is the Renaissance. During this time people in the West began doubting publicly things that formerly were not doubted. One of these was the assumption that such a God exists. By 1600 there were quite a few agnostics and atheists in Europe. To deal with these doubters, René Descartes proposed a new foundation for knowledge: 'Cogito, ergo sum!' His proposal proved to be one of the most influential statements in the history of philosophy.

"You may not be familiar with his exact wording. It's Latin, the language of scholars in those days. It means, 'I think, therefore I am.' He was saying that because he could think, he was confident that he existed. You see, he was trying to figure out

René Descartes (day KART)
(1596–1650)

some way to communicate with people who didn't believe in God and who therefore didn't have the foundation for epistemology that premoderns had. So he asked himself, 'What is the one thing that I cannot doubt?' His answer was that he could not doubt that he existed so long as he was a thinker who was thinking."

"Why not just say, 'I see myself in the mirror, therefore I am'?"

"Because that can be doubted," Carla answered. "Our eyes can play tricks on us. We've all seen things that turned out not to exist. Descartes acknowledged this and said that the operation of an individual mind is the only solid foundation for epistemology. *Because I think, I can be confident that I exist.* On that basis Descartes intended to build a system of arguments that would prove the existence of God and the legitimacy of the Christian faith to atheists and agnostics."

"And this changed the world?" Brad asked suspiciously.

"Yes, it certainly did—or at least it *coincided* with a change in the development of Western philosophy. You see, premoderns took the existence of God and His communication to man as their foundation for knowledge: *I know because God knows all and has spoken to man.* But, with the influential work of Descartes, moderns tended to take the reasoning capacity of the individual knower as the foundation of knowledge. *I know because I can think; or, I know something is true because it is reasonable.* The foundation for knowing was no longer God but the individual human knower."

Modern Epistemology

"Did Descartes succeed?" I asked.

"Yes and no. He succeeded in convincing almost everyone that something other than God and the Bible should be the foundation of all knowledge. He failed, however, to convince people that this starting point should be human reason. He also failed to convince people that any foundation for knowledge could lead to belief in God and the Christian religion.

"In considering what happened after Descartes, I don't want to get bogged down in too many details. What you need to remember is that from roughly 1650 to the late 1900s, Western philosophy agreed with Descartes that a foundation for knowledge was necessary, and they more or less agreed that this foundation should be reason."

"But we're not in the late 1900s anymore, so I guess Western philosophy is different now?" I asked.

"For the most part, yes—very different. And this is due to a number of factors, not the least of which was the philosophy of Friedrich Nietzsche. Nietzsche (who died in 1900) was quite different from most of the thinkers who preceded him. He was an outspoken atheist, and he called into question the whole idea of knowledge. He was about as different from Descartes as a philosopher can be and still be a philosopher. He rejected the idea that reason was the foundation for all knowledge—in fact he denied that there was a foundation for knowledge. He claimed that what we view as knowledge is only a human creation. Language is not the communication of real ideas; it is only an endless circle of interpretation. Nietzsche also rejected the idea of universal morality. He thought that morality differed profoundly from one person to another. In the end, Nietzsche denied that there was any discernable unity

Friedrich Nietzsche (NEE chuh) denied that reason was the foundation for knowledge and thus undermined modernity's view of epistemology.

to the world, and he believed that humans have no access to reality whatsoever.

"Now, that's how we got to the twentieth century. In the decades following Nietzsche's death, Western philosophers tended to be, like Nietzsche, boldly atheistic. But unlike Nietzsche they seemed convinced that it was possible to know reality through reason and the scientific method. By the middle of the century much of the earth's population was ruled by governments taking this view of the world."

"Communism, right?" I asked.

"Right. And from here you should know the story pretty well. By the 1970s the legitimacy of Communism was being questioned throughout the West. One reason was that European— especially French—philosophers had begun to see the epistemological problems that Communism had. It denied that there was any convincing proof for the existence of God. But it failed to realize that its belief in Marxism and the progress of the human race had no more proof. Another reason was that Communism's flagship regime, the Soviet Union, was frighteningly cruel. Evidence of shocking atrocities kept pouring out of the Soviet Union until even liberal European and American philosophers became unsympathetic with Marxism."

"And, of course," Brad added, "the collapse of the Soviet Union in the early 1990s didn't help."

"That was, I suppose, the final nail in the coffin. It was a sad day for the humanists of the world. Marxism was a philosophy of history for a huge segment of the West. It was a religion of sorts for them. The fall of Communism represented their loss of hope. Theistic philosophy lost its foundation for knowledge through the Enlightenment and the Age of Reason. Atheistic philosophy lost its foundation for knowledge in the late twentieth century. History now seemed to have no goal. Once again, the world had lost its center. Just as premodernity had given way to modernity, so now modernity gave way to postmodernity.

"Now, at the beginning of this historical survey, I told you that I see myself as playing an active role in a major epistemological shift in the history of the West. Well, this is that shift—the move from modernism to postmodernism."

"Postmodernism. OK, so what is it?" I had been waiting to ask this question for a very, very long time.

Carla paused for a moment and then spoke. "That's a hard question to answer. The word is used in many different ways. It can refer to certain kinds of architecture, art, and entertainment."

"Well, I guess we'd be interested in the postmodernism that refers to philosophy," I said.

"Yes, of course. But even there we find some significant disagreement. What I'll do is tell you about the kind of philosophical postmodernism that I most agree with—which in my understanding is also the most influential kind."

"OK, let's hear it," Brad said.

"Postmodernism is basically a rejection of modernism," Carla began.

"And what, again, is modernism?" I was very glad Brad asked that.

"Well, that is very hard to answer too. But I think I can capture the

> *Postmodernism is basically a rejection of modernism.*

essence of it by describing it in terms of epistemology. Modernism is a worldview that, with Descartes, takes reason as its foundation for knowledge. Now, of course, experience and the scientific method figure in too, as a sort of help to reason. I guess the best expression of it would be Ted's mantra: 'Reason informed by science is the only way to know that something is true.' "

"And rejecting this as the foundation for knowledge is what postmodernism is all about?" That was my question.

"No, not really. There is something even more basic. Postmodernism also involves a rejection of modernism's ontology."

"Postmodernism has a special view of cancer?"

Carla laughed. "You're thinking of *oncology,* the study of tumors. I said *ontology,* the study of the nature of being. It's not just that postmoderns don't view knowledge like moderns. They also don't view the nature of being in the same way. And this difference really is the fundamental distinction between modernism and postmodernism.

"Boy, this stuff just gets weirder and weirder."

"I'm with you, Brad. Weird."

"Modernism thinks of the world as a unified place," Carla began again.

"How so?" I asked.

"It thinks that there is an all-inclusive system of explanations that tells people where the world came from, why it exists, and what it will one day become."

"And postmoderns don't?" I asked that.

"No. The world just isn't like that. It's not single or unified. It's fractured and contradictory. Any attempt to put all the pieces together produces harm, not good. *All attempts to construct a metanarrative are misguided and should be abandoned.* I guess you could say that that statement is the fundamental tenet of postmodernism."

"Metanarrative?"

"In this context I'm defining a *narrative* as the story of something's existence. Everyone has a narrative. You have a narrative, your family has a narrative, your school has a narrative, your country has a narrative. *Meta* means 'beyond.' So what I'm saying is that there is no single narrative beyond all narratives, into which every other narrative fits. Now this conclusion can be verified from history. Every attempt to construct a metanarrative has failed. Take Christianity and

Communism. Christianity's metanarrative states that God made the world, that the world rebelled, but that He has a plan to redeem the world through His Son. Well, two thousand years ago His Son came to earth, taught His people how to live, died for the sins of the world, and then went back to heaven. The problem is that His people never lived the way He told them to. The metanarrative promised heaven on earth; it in fact delivered oppression and hate."

"And Communism?"

"Just as bad. It claimed that the universe had always existed and that mankind was earth's most advanced being. As the most advanced being, man must continue the universe's evolution by freeing human society from religious faith and ensuring the growth of human knowledge. Again, the result was a complete failure. It promised freedom, equality, and progress. It delivered just the opposite."

"And this proves that—"

"That the ontological understanding of the modernists is very problematic. The world is not unified by a single set of all-inclusive explanations. There is no metanarrative."

"OK, well, we spent a lot of time talking about epistemology. How does modernism's epistemology fit into this ontology stuff?" If it turned out that all of Carla's talk about epistemology didn't matter, I was going to scream.

"Because I reject modernism's ontology, I also reject its epistemology. The key modernistic thinkers assumed that the world was a unified thing, and they therefore assumed that some foundation for knowledge existed. If some unifying purpose is woven into the fabric of the universe, then there must be some way for us to discover that purpose. Based on that assumption, Descartes and others proposed *reason* as that way—as the foundation for knowledge."

"But since there is no unity in the world, there's no reason to think that a foundation for knowing the world exists," I said, basically just thinking out loud.

Carla followed up immediately: "Since there is no unity, no foundation is possible. The whole idea of a single foundation assumes that what is to be constructed is singular and unified. A single concrete slab cannot serve as a foundation for a tri-level in Michigan, a double-wide in Georgia, and a two-story villa in Spain. Because the structure is not singular, the foundation cannot be singular.

"I think you will find that history supports what I am saying. Descartes sought a foundation for knowing, but all he really did was start philosophy on its very unsatisfying attempt to answer the question, 'How can I know that I know?' "

"Do you have a satisfying answer?" Brad asked.

"Yes—one that satisfies me at least."

"Let's hear it."

"No."

"No what?"

"No, there is no way to know that you know something."

"And that satisfies you?"

"Absolutely. It frees me from trying to accomplish what I cannot do. Namely, find a foundation for knowledge. You could call me a confident *antifoundationalist*. I reject foundationalism, the idea that knowledge rests on a set of beliefs that cannot be doubted. Ah, yes. Let me tell you, it is a liberating feeling."

Postmodern Epistemology

"So you never use the words *know* or *knowledge?*" I asked.

"Oh, I use them all right. But my understanding of the words is different from the modernist's."

The Tenets of Postmodernism

I. Rejection of Modernism's Ontology

II. Rejection of Modernism's Epistemology
   A. Rejection of the certainty of knowledge
   B. Rejection of the objectivity of knowledge
   C. Rejection of the goodness of knowledge

"Well, you'll have to tell us your meaning, because from the sound of it, we're much closer to modernism than postmodernism." That was Brad's statement, though I was thinking it too.

"Postmodernism rejects the three basic modernistic assumptions regarding knowledge. It denies that knowledge is certain, objective, and that it is necessarily good."

"So when you say that you know something, you don't mean that you are certain it's true?" I asked.

"Right. Knowledge is a humanly constructed image; it is not something that corresponds to reality. Knowing is like look-

Knowledge is Certain

ing at a drawing of an atom. What you see is not actually an atom but a *model* that has been made to look like what we think an atom—the structure of which no one has ever seen—looks like."

"Weird. OK, let's test your idea. I *know* that George Washington was America's first president. So are you trying to tell me that that fact is just an image—that it's not certain he was the first president?"

"That's right, Brad. And it's because there's no foundation for knowledge. Haven't you been listening?"

"Well, of course I have," Brad answered right away. "And, yes, your statement about the foundation for knowledge is *very* familiar by now, but I was wondering—"

"Brad, if there is no foundation for knowledge, then knowledge cannot be certain—just as a house without a foundation cannot be stable. Let me deal with it this way: Why do you think that you know for certain that George Washington was the first president?"

"Because everybody says so. All of today's history books say so, stuff written back then says so, and a bunch of people between then and now have said so."

"And to you it would be completely unreasonable to suppose that he was not, right?"

"Exactly! It would be totally unreasonable."

"I agree."

"Carla, you can't agree—you're a postmodernist! You think that knowledge isn't certain."

"But I do agree. It is only reasonable to say that George Washington was the first president. My point, however, is that reason is not the foundation for knowledge. So the fact that what you say about George Washington is reasonable doesn't mean that it's certain. I'll even say that I *know* that George Washington was the first president. I will not, however, say that that means it's certain."

"Carla, if something is reasonable, it is certain."

"And that, Brad, would make you a modernist. You evidently believe that reason is the foundation for knowledge."

"Well, maybe I do. Why don't you?"

"For one thing, reason is not universal. What is reasonable to one person isn't to another. Let's move away from George Washington for now. His historicity is not controversial, so he isn't a good example anymore. Let's talk about Communism. This is a system based on the assumption that government should control the wealth in society, redistributing it so that all people are equal. Hence, the sacred mantra of Communism: 'From each according to his ability; to each according to his need.' Pursuing such an ideal, say the Communists, will lead to utopia. The poor will have their needs met, and the rich will be saved from the corruption that results from having wealth. Pretty reasonable, eh?"

It was all I could do to stay in my seat. "No way, Carla. All that does is reward laziness and punish hard work. What ends up happening is everyone becomes poor because people know that if they work hard they can't keep what they make, and if they don't work, their needs will still be met."

"Hmm. You sound like a capitalist."

"How could a reasonable person be anything else?" I said in triumph.

"And here we begin to come to the point—what is reasonable to one person is not to another. A capitalist attempting to enter a Russian university in 1979 would have been scorned for the reasoning you just employed. His fellow Russians would have thrown away his application without considering it. But if an American in 1979 heard about this outspoken Russian capitalist, he would have come to a completely different conclusion. The American would have concluded that that same reasoning was a sure sign of remarkable intelligence."

"Well, it's obvious *now* who's right," Brad answered. "No one believes in Communism anymore. You just can't deny that capitalism is a better way. Communism has fallen apart."

"There are still many Communists in the world, and many powerful politicians even in America would still defend the mantra that I quoted a few minutes ago."

"But what could they say about the fall of the Soviet Union and the poverty of the North Koreans?"

"The same thing you would say if the American economy fell apart. They would say that people failed the system, not that the system failed the people—or something like that. They would be incapable of questioning the system itself. That would be against reason as they know it. Now please don't get me wrong. I'm not opposed to using reason in the construction of knowledge. But you have to understand that what results is not something that's certain. And that is my point—*knowledge is not certain.*"

"OK, let's go back to George Washington. So you wouldn't tell a group of first graders that George was the first president?"

"Of course I would! Just as a chemistry teacher would tell a group of eleventh graders that a drawing of an atom is an atom. George Washington as the first president is a model—a useful fiction. It fits our social context well and helps us function in the community where we find ourselves.

"Ah, yes. And this brings me to postmodernism's second rejection of modernity's epistemology. Postmodernism denies that knowledge is objective. Modernism's commitment to the objectivity of knowledge goes all the way back to Descartes. You can hear it in his famous statement: 'I think, therefore I am.' The emphasis is on *I*, the individual knower. To the modernist, knowledge is possible only when the knower strips himself of his historical background, his personal convictions, and his philosophical commitments. He is to be a dispassionate observer. He must stand outside the historical process as an unconditioned specialist. Then and only then, says the modernist, can knowledge be possible—because knowledge must be objective."

Knowledge is Objective

"And you think this is impossible."

"Yes. But I also think it's undesirable. You see, our background and our emotions are not the enemy. They actually help us and motivate us in the process of discovery."

"Well, I've got to know more about these 'convictions and commitments,' " Brad said. "It seems to me that we can let go of them."

"Two things need to be said. First, we must realize the role that community plays in the production of knowledge. Second, we must realize that a desire for power inevitably colors our thinking in the production of knowledge.

"All right. Let's start with the community thing. Knowledge is culturally based; it is socially constructed. We cannot rise above the human communities that have produced us."

"And why not?" Brad again.

"Because all human systems (for example, language, logic, and morality) are social constructions. That's the reason that the Russians and Americans in the previous illustration could not understand each other. Each is produced by a different community that defines reason differently. We'd like to think that all human systems are *referential*—that they refer to objects in reality. But they are not; they are instead *reflexive*. They don't refer to reality; they just point back to themselves. They point back to the communities that have framed them."

"OK, how about an example?"

"This is perhaps best seen in interpretation of texts. Do you have any idea how difficult it is to get two people from different communities to agree on the interpretation of a text? Take, for example, a freshman literature course at a typical university. The teacher reads a poem by John Donne and then asks Susie from Illinois to tell the class what she thinks it means. Then the teacher asks Abdul from Saudi Arabia, and then Jean-Louis from France, and then finally Katie from southern California. Each gives a radically different interpretation. And I say that's because each is the product of a radically different community."

"Aaaaaagh! Carla, you don't figure out a poem by listening to what different readers think about it. You're supposed to find out what the *author meant*." I was impressed. Brad was holding his own pretty well—for the moment at least.

"Brad, who's to say that knowing what the author meant is the goal of interpretation? That poem—or any text—does not have its origin in the author's intentions or his thoughts. The community that produced the author produced his thoughts and therefore his poem. The poem does not refer to reality—only to the human systems that the community has chosen to construct. Consider that famous sentence from the Declaration of Independence: 'We hold these truths to be self-evident, that all men are created equal, that they are endowed by their Creator with certain unalienable rights, that among these are Life, Liberty, and the pursuit of Happiness.' So what does that mean?"

"That all men are equal and therefore should be free," Brad answered.

"Well, that's not interpreting according to the author's intent. That doesn't seem to be how Thomas Jefferson viewed things. He owned slaves when he wrote that."

"So what is the goal of interpreting?"

"To show what I have just shown. That all texts are filled with contradictions." Truly a stunning statement by Carla.

"Why interpret anything then?" I asked.

"A text—whether a poem, a narrative, or a philosophical treatise—is a stage where people from different communities can get together and express their ideas. No interpretation can legitimately be said to have certain and final authority. The way that human language works just doesn't allow for that approach. Human language is not human communication. It is the ever-contradictory interaction of ideas."

"How can you live with that view?" Brad asked.

"I think I probably enjoy life with my understanding more than you do with yours. Realizing that knowledge is not objective—that it is determined by one's community—is a good thing. It allows us to see that our only source for guidance is the inheritance we have received from our fellow humans and the conversations we endeavor to maintain with them. This realization encourages us to focus on *conversation* with other communities, rather than *confrontation*. We shouldn't be trying to change other people's minds. We should be learning to appreciate the beauty of the way their communities have taught them to think."

"Whew!" Honestly, that was all I could think to say. I guess that was my community training coming through.

"Now let's talk about the second reason I think knowledge cannot be viewed as objective. Every knower is motivated to some extent by a desire for power. The modernist assumes that knowledge can be objective because he thinks it's possible for a person to interact with the world dispassionately—with only his intellect. But any honest thinker has to admit that one's emotions and desires inevitably intrude. This is where the writings of Michel Foucault become very important.

"He asserted that knowledge and power are tied together. Knowledge is constructed and communicated as a means of exerting power over other people and things. People seek and spread knowledge not because they sense a need for 'truth' but because they want power—whether they realize it or not. That's why Jefferson and his community produced the Declaration of Independence. Together they held up the ideal of liberty—that all people are equal and therefore should be free—not because it was 'the truth.' Their own contradictory behavior demonstrates that. They fabricated the 'self-evident' ideal of liberty as an exertion of power. They wanted to be released from Britain's power so that they could exert their own. All 'knowledge,' whether it concerns ethics or particle physics, is about power."

"Particle physics too?!" Brad exclaimed. "Oh, c'mon, Carla, don't be a cynic. We study particle physics because that's just the way the world is. We go to school to learn how the world works. Particle physics is an important part of that. So we learn about particle physics."

"Particle physics is in your high school curriculum because scientists and governments in the early twentieth century wanted to blow people up. Our knowledge of the atom exists largely because we wanted to win a war."

"Well, that's just an isolated example. This knowledge has also been used to give electricity and comfort to millions of people. That's a good thing."

"It's still the desire for power though—power over nature for the sake of our own comfort. And what do you think would happen to particle physics if some discovery made all study of the atom useless for national defense and the production of electricity?"

"Dunno."

"No more particle physics. Governments and wealthy investors would stop funding the research, and eventually there would be no more search for or communication of knowledge concerning particle physics."

"That'd be cool." Seemed like the right thing for me to say at the moment. "OK, so what does this prove?"

"That the desire for power is fundamental to the production and communication of knowledge. No power (or prospect of power), no knowledge. Well, obviously, given this situation, you cannot expect knowledge to ever be objective."

"All right, Carla," I said. "Let's try to wrap this up pretty soon. Didn't you say there was something else that you reject about modernism's epistemology?"

"Postmodernism denies that knowledge is necessarily good. As you could tell from Ted's talk, education is a very important thing for modernists. We must flood our society with knowledge and then train individuals to think and reason correctly. A better society, they say, is then sure to result. More knowledge is bound to produce a better world."

"Not true, evidently?"

"If the twentieth century teaches us anything, it tells us that knowledge can be a very bad thing. Technology often does as much harm as it does good, and sometimes its harmful effects far outweigh its benefits. When we learned how to split the atom, we opened the door to nuclear holocaust and the problem of dealing with a dangerous new kind of nondisposable waste. Who knows what dangers we will face because of what we are now learning about the human genetic structure?"

"So we should stop learning, stop going to school?" Brad asked.

"No, of course not. We should realize, however, that it is not enough just to grow in knowledge. We must also grow in *respect.* We must learn to respect our fellow human beings. All human communities, no matter how different from our own, are valuable—are *beautiful.* Gaining this respect will help to keep us from being abusive with our knowledge."

"Now, Carla," Brad began, "all of what you've said has been pretty interesting, but it's also been very theoretical. You've told us how postmodernism thinks. But I think we should also know what postmodernism *does.* Does postmodernism have a mission?"

"Yes. To expose modernism."

"Really?"

"Absolutely."

"But aren't you also looking to make a better world?"

"No. Not right away at least. We first must demonstrate that the status quo has problems. Only then can we move on to the positive side."

"And what about modernism do you want to expose?"

"That it cannot live up to its claims. That there is no foundation for knowledge. That modernistic ontology is indefensible. That modernistic epistemology must be rejected. That knowledge is not certain, is not objective, and is not necessarily good. That—"

"OK, OK, OK! We've been there already, Carla." I thought that if I had to go through any of that stuff again, my brain would explode. "I think our question right now is *how* do you propose to make your case?"

"By proving that it is the margins that constitute the text."

Postmodernism wishes to expose modernism by proving that it is the margins that constitute the text.

"Yet another completely useless statement." Brad.

"Think about a page from a book. Where is the text on the page—crammed in the top right corner, squished along the left edge of the page?"

"No, it's in the center," I said.

"Right. And how do you know it's centered on the page?"

"I guess because there's a consistent margin all around it that frames the text on the page." Me again.

"That's how life works too. And it is my purpose in life—or at least one of them—to critique cultural units (accepted ideals, institutions, and personalities) by demonstrating that it is the 'margins' that place the 'text' in the center of the cultural page. You see, these units are not legitimized by actual appeals to truth but by an active process of exclusion, opposition, and repression."

"We're going to need an example." Brad.

"Take the ideal of individualism, a favorite in American culture. This is the belief in the primary importance of the individual and in the virtues of self-reliance and personal independence. When a person holds up this idea as good, he is engaging in an

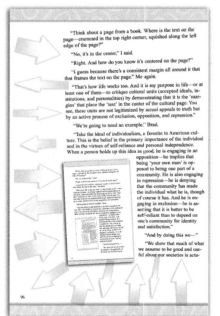

opposition—he implies that being 'your own man' is opposed to being one part of a community. He is also engaging in repression—he is denying that the community has made the individual what he is, though of course it has. And he is engaging in exclusion—he is asserting that it is better to be self-reliant than to depend on one's community for identity and satisfaction."

"And by doing this we—"

"We show that much of what we assume to be good and useful about our societies is actually false, unstable, and even immoral. We also end up discovering that there are some very important ideas, institutions, and people that we have repressed and excluded. And we learn that we should be removing them from the 'margin' and placing them at the 'center.' "

"OK, well, this is still pretty fuzzy in my mind. Umm, are there any movements or groups in society that you think are doing a good job with this margin-to-the-center thing?" Brad asked.

"I'll mention three: multiculturalism, the gay rights movement, and feminism. Gay rights and feminism represent two classes of people who have traditionally been opposed, repressed, and excluded in the West. These movements—for the most part—do an admirable job of attempting to take these 'margins' and bring them to the center of the 'text' of society. Multiculturalism is similar, but instead of dealing with marginalized groups within the West, it deals with cultures in the world that the West has marginalized. It endeavors to show that there are communities all over the world that the West has wrongly tried either to ignore or to change. It also shows that these cultures have a beauty and an authenticity that ought not to be tampered with. They are valuable and viable as they are."

Key Postmodern Movements

- Multiculturalism
- Gay rights
- Feminism

"And what else?" I was really hoping that this was the end.

"Well, of course, I could go on for hours, but—"

"I think you already have." Brad, naturally.

"But that's all that really needs to be said, I think," Carla finally concluded.

"OK, Brad, shall we open it up for the eggheads?"

"Be my guest."

Salvadore Dali's The Ghost of Vermeer of Delft Which Can Be Used as a Table *(1934) anticipates in art postmodernism's rejection of absolute standards of rationality.*

Can We Live with No Foundation?

8

Memory Verses: Romans 1:22–25

It only seemed right to give Ted dibs on grilling Carla. "Ted, do you have anything to say?" I asked.

"I guess the thing that intrigued me most about your presentation, Carla, was what you said about knowledge not being objective."

"I know that goes against your grain, Ted, but sooner or later we all have to face the fact that objectivity in knowledge just is not possible. I, like you, grew up thinking it was possible. But I later learned that objectivity assumes a foundation for knowledge, and it does not reckon with the fact that knowledge is culturally based. We cannot rise—"

"—Rise above the human communities that have produced us," Ted finished her sentence. "Yes, I was listening. And the reason you gave for this was that logic is socially constructed. Is that right?"

"Right. Contrary to your thinking, I don't view logic as providing us with an unobstructed view of the truth. It's like a painting painted by a blind man; it's not a lens clearly focused on the truth. But it's more than logic that I'm talking about here. It's *all human systems.* That would include language. Human language is not communication. This is the reason I'm opposed to making the author's intent the goal of interpretation. Understanding what the author meant to communicate is not possible in interpretation, and it is not desirable. Now, Ted, I recognize that this is diffi—"

"Uh, Carla, I hate to interrupt, but I think I really need a glass of water. Would you please get me one?"

Certainly seemed like an odd request, but Carla didn't appear to mind. She left the table and within a minute returned with water for Ted. I must admit it was touching to see these two, who obviously had big philosophical differences, acting like friends.

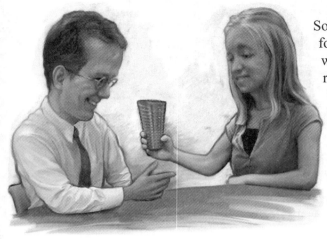

Sort of gave me hope for world peace. It was a hope that died right after it was born.

"Carla, why in the world did you just do that?"

"Do what?"

"Give me a glass of water."

"Because you said you wanted one!"

"Well, I know that's what I said, but that's not what I meant. I meant for you to tell me more about your understanding of ontology."

"Ted, you are weirder than anyone gives you credit for."

"No weirder than you suppose all of us to be, Carla." And I thought this part of the discussion was going to be boring! Ted continued: "You say that the goal of interpretation is not the author's intent, because knowing intent is neither possible nor is it desirable. But I've just disproved both.

"It is desirable to know the author's intent—no conversation can be possible without it. If asking for water actually means asking for more on ontology, then the meaningful discussion that we've had around this table could not have happened. I have also demonstrated that knowing the author's intent is possible. All of us—including you—assume that all the time, and that assumption is verified by our daily experience. I surprised everyone at the table just now by asserting that my meaning was impossible to determine from my wording—that I didn't really want water. You responded to my claim (my claim that I actually wanted a discussion of ontology) by concluding that I was weird—that I must be an absurd thinker. And you're right. Only a crazy person would use human language in a way that didn't communicate. But you know what? I was kidding. I really did want water! Thanks—and thanks for helping me make my point." With that, Ted took a long drink from the glass that Carla gave him.

"Ted, you're just having a hard time forsaking your worn-out worldview. You are stuck in an unworkable modernistic epistemology."

Ted looked down at his glass and spoke with a smile: "Carla, I'm so glad you've come around to my way of thinking."

"I am not coming around to your way of thinking!"

"Well, that's how I'm reading you when you say, 'You're stuck in an unworkable modernistic epistemology.' After all, human systems (like language and logic) are not *referential*. They are *reflexive*. Your *words* spoke of my worldview as unworkable, but I know that those words weren't *referring* to anything in *reality*. They were only pointing back to the community that produced you. Since it's not possible to know any author's intended meaning, I'm just using your 'text' as a stage on which to display the thinking of my community. I really was hoping that you would respond by attempting to appreciate the beauty of the way my community has taught me to think."

"I refuse to appreciate a 'community' that is ridiculing my thinking." Carla was not happy.

"And how do you know that I'm ridiculing you? You're not trying to interpret my statements according to my intended meaning, are you?"

"Ted, I admit that we are able to communicate with a high level of understanding because the two of us come from the same community. If, howev—"

"Oh, so we're from the same community, are we? Well, as I listened to you rage against modernism, I felt pretty sure that you didn't agree very much at all with people you call 'modernists'— people like me. Judging from your presentation, I'd say we're from very different communities. And yet we still understand each other, don't we? I *know* that Ravi and Li come from communities quite different than yours. Yet you've had meaningful interaction with them too around this table.

"You know, Carla, that brings up another important point. You said that it's not possible for us to rise above the communities that have produced us. But the fact is that people do change communities. That's what you've done. You were raised in a more-or-less modernistic context, but somehow you got convinced to leave it. Doesn't this prove that there is something about logic that transcends one's community? Logic can't be constructed by each community if people from different communities can communicate and sometimes even convince one another."

"But still, Ted, we cannot say that knowledge is objective."

"Why not? If I can listen to a speech or read a book and understand the author's intended meaning, then I can know something objectively. It's not *my* meaning that I've discovered; it's the *author's*. It's therefore not subjective; it's objective. If I can do that in interpreting texts, why can't I do it in other endeavors too?"

"But, Ted, you're just not reckoning with the profound effect that one's community has on the knowing process."

"Not to mention the effect that the desire for power has," Jack inserted, surprising everyone.

"Yes, that's right," Carla said. "Wait a minute, Jack, you're not supposed to agree with me, are you?"

"Well, I agree that Ted doesn't reckon with the difficulty of maintaining objectivity in the knowing process. In fact, in a way I don't think you have reckoned with the difficulty of it."

"What?!" said Carla, Ted, Ravi, Li, Brad, Guide Girl, and I.

"As a Christian," Jack continued, "I am acutely aware of the difficulty humans have in knowing something objectively. And the problem, as I see it, is far more profound than one's community and the desire for power. *Sin* is also a huge factor. The Bible teaches that all humans are sinners, unwilling to face the truth about themselves and the holy God who made them. 'The heart is deceitful above all things, and desperately wicked: who can know it?' That's what God has to say about mankind and epistemology. We're so evil that we cannot even know ourselves. So the idea that we can be dispassionate observers—that we must stand outside the historical process as unconditioned specialists—is to me totally unacceptable."

"Well, this is certainly unexpected," Carla said. "So you would agree that knowledge cannot be objective or certain?"

"No."

"No?! You have to come to that conclusion, Jack. If the barriers to objectivity are even greater than I've said, then you have to agree with me."

"No, I don't. I think your conclusion is extreme. We do face huge obstacles in the knowing process, but experience tells all of us that certain and objective knowledge is possible."

"Not as I see it. Experience teaches me that objectivity and certainty are impossible. Whether you're talking about interpreting the Declaration of Independence or studying particle physics, we just don't know what we think we know. People in Jefferson's time thought he meant freedom for rich white males. But people in the North during the Civil War said he was talking about black people as well as white people. And it wasn't until much after the Civil War that anybody thought 'all men are created equal' referred to Native Americans. And when it comes to studying the atom . . . well, let me just say that nearly everything that physicists 'knew' about the atom a century ago, they now no longer 'know.' "

"In my mind, Carla, what you're saying does not challenge the idea of certainty or objectivity in knowing."

"Jack, I just don't know how you can say that."

"You are presenting us with an age-old logical fallacy—what many people call the

*Postmodernism often engages in the **either-or** fallacy.*

either-or fallacy. What you're saying is, *Either* we know something completely, exhaustively, and absolutely, *or* we do not know it at all. Well, of course, you can always disprove the 'either' clause. If I say that Jefferson *meant* to include African slaves and Native Americans in his famous statement, you can always counter that he owned slaves and never evidenced a concern for the plight of the Indians. If, however, I say that Jefferson *meant* to exclude those two people groups in the Declaration of Independence, then you could say that he may have intended them too but that he didn't act like it because he knew that his fellow Americans were not ready for that yet.

"So, yes, I agree that I cannot know what Thomas Jefferson meant exhaustively or absolutely. But I refuse to think that my only other choice is to say that I am lost in a befuddling wilderness of dangerous uncertainty—that I cannot know for certain anything that Jefferson meant. There is no simple 'either-or' here. I have another choice: I can say that I know what he meant *to a degree.* I know that he was at least arguing for the freedom of aristocratic white males in the American colonies."

"Well, that's not very much."

"I'd say that's quite a bit," Jack answered. "It's all I really need to know to understand the significance of the Declaration of Independence in that time period. The same goes for particle physics. It is true that much has changed in this area, but you yourself admitted that not everything has been overturned. You said, '*Nearly* everything that physicists "knew," they now no longer "know." ' So evidently at least some of what they 'knew' they truly knew. Furthermore, if we can know nothing for certain, on what basis can we claim that previous theories have been overturned? Carla, what I'm saying is that there are degrees in knowing. And knowledge does not have to be exhaustive to be true knowledge. Certainly this is something that our daily experience bears witness to—as Ted's harsh but effective trick has demonstrated quite well."

"But it seems to me that your Christianity wouldn't allow for this. Isn't it true that if I can't know even my own heart, I can know nothing?"

"OK, you're referring to the biblical condemnation about the human heart, 'Who can know it?' Well, I think this should not be understood in an absolute sense. God isn't saying that we cannot know *anything* about ourselves. He is saying that we cannot know ourselves completely—particularly the extent of our own depravity. But God certainly expects humans to know many things. Take, for example, what Jesus Christ said to some of the Jews of His day."

Jack pulled out what looked like a very small black Bible. "I think it's in the sixteenth chapter of Matthew," he said as he flipped through the pages. "Yes, here it is. Listen to this.

> The Pharisees also with the Sadducees came, and tempting desired him [that is, Jesus] that he would shew them a sign from heaven. He answered and said unto them, When it is evening, ye say, It will be fair weather: for the sky is red. And in the morning, It will be foul weather to day: for the sky is red and lowring. O ye hypocrites, ye can discern the face of the sky; but can ye not discern the signs of the times?"

"Hmm," Brad broke his long silence. "Not the sort of Bible lesson one would expect from Jack. Any connection to what's been said?"

"Yes, absolutely," Jack answered. "You see, long before Christ came to earth, mankind had learned—through reason and a primitive kind of scientific method—that a red sky in the morning indicated bad weather ahead. Despite all the barriers that humans face in the knowing process, Christ did not question that these Jews truly knew there was a cause-effect relationship between a red sky and bad weather. In fact, He rebukes them for not knowing more. He asserts that since they could figure out one aspect of earth science, they should have figured out one aspect of 'God-science' (or theology)—that God had sent His Son into the world and that He was that Son.

"Anyway, Carla, my point is that Christianity—even with its severe statements about human epistemology—does still allow for the certainty and objectivity of knowledge."

"In fact," began Ravi, "when all is said and done, I think we must conclude that even Carla believes that knowledge is certain."

"Really?!" Carla said weakly. She'd been through a lot. I half expected her to ask for some protein blaster, but then I thought that doing so would just remind everyone of her fiasco with Ted. She never asked for anything.

"Carla," Ravi continued, "you have condemned modernism for being arrogant and overly confident about knowing. But you have

Postmodernism does believe in certainty of knowledge: it "knows" that knowledge cannot be certain.

shown a similar arrogance. You think so hard about thinking that you arrogantly claim that knowledge (traditionally understood) is not possible. You are convinced that we cannot be convinced. You know that we cannot know. Thus, you admit that you do know something for certain—*that knowing cannot be certain!*"

For once, Carla was silent.

That's when Guide spoke up: "Uh, Li, you're the only one that hasn't participated in this examination of Carla's views. Do you have anything to add, or anything to ask?"

"Yes, I do. Carla, you said that morality, like language and logic, is a human system and that it is just a social construction. Frankly, I find this very disturbing, and I think it makes your worldview unlivable. We simply cannot live in a world that allows each community to make up its own laws of morality."

"Why not? I believe that I do."

"*9-11-01.* Does that date have any meaning for you?"

"Obviously, that was a very great tragedy, but—"

"How can you, with your worldview, say that it was a tragedy? It was simply the clash of two communities, each with a different definition of morality. The United States had constructed its own moral laws, and so had the radical Muslims gathered around Osama bin Laden. There was nothing dark or evil about what the terrorists did. They were just following the dictates of their own community. Their own *beautiful* culture!"

"Certainly what the terrorists did that day was not 'beautiful,' " Carla was quick to answer. "September 11 *was* a tragedy, and there's nothing in my worldview that keeps me from saying that. In fact, if more people in the West had my worldview, I think what happened that day could have been avoided. If Americans had been more committed to multiculturalism, these 'radical Muslims' (as you called them) would not have felt so ostracized and abused by us. Instead of belittling them over the past decade or two, we could have been interacting with them—showing them that each community has something valuable to contribute to the world."

The forever-changed skyline of New York City stands as a monument to postmodernism's inability to account for universal moral laws.

"Li, you are definitely right," Jack began. "This is a very important point. Carla, you have claimed that there is nothing universal or transcendent about morality—that ethics and moral laws are merely social constructions. But, Carla, there is no way that you can live with this view."

"I can and I do."

"You can't and I know for a fact that you don't. Your point about knowledge not being good and your point about 'bringing the margins to the center' both reveal that you believe in at least one universal moral law. You are convinced that no one should be marginalized. You believe it is wrong to repress or exclude anyone. That is a moral belief, and it is a belief that you wish to apply universally. Part of the agenda of feminism, the gay rights movement, and multiculturalism is to go into other communities and change their thinking about those they have repressed or excluded. You have demonstrated that by what you've said about the Islamic extremists and the September 11 attacks."

"No, I refuse to be a part of this power play. You're just using your understanding of logic and 'truth' to force me into your mold. This is the sort of thing that Michel Foucault spoke of again and again. This discussion isn't about 'truth' and 'knowledge.' It's about getting power over other people and maintaining the status quo. Well, I'm not going to play that game."

"What game will you play then?" Jack asked. It was plain to me that Jack was not simply trying to win a debate, like Ted. He seemed like he was really trying to help Carla think through these important issues.

"What do you mean?"

"If your worldview is correct, then no matter what we do, we're ultimately just playing someone's game. And let me tell you, you do not want to play Foucault's game."

"And why not?"

"He's dead."

"As are most philosophers, Jack."

"But he died early, at the height of his writing career. And you know why, don't you?"

"He died of AIDS. Jack, please don't try to make something of this. It's cruel, and you'll only embarrass yourself."

"Carla, I will make something of this, and no one should take it as cruel. Discussing philosophy often has an edge to it because we're talking about our most cherished beliefs. Once we have chosen to seek answers to ultimate questions in a public debate, we have chosen to hear some things that will make us uncomfortable."

At this point Jack started addressing all of us at the table. "In the tradition of Nietzsche, Foucault claimed that what we view as knowledge is only a human creation. He denied that there was a universal morality. He thought that morality differed profoundly from one person to another. He therefore viewed the moral pronouncements of religion as nothing more than an exertion of power. The religious claim that certain actions are 'sin' is not a revelation of true morality, he said. It is a power play—an attempt to regulate the behavior of others by a fabrication, an 'invention of truth.' Foucault flaunted his rebellion against this 'power play' by giving

Michel (mee SHEL) Foucault (foo KOH) died on June 25, 1984, a victim of his own philosophy.

free reign to his homosexual impulses. After several years of this kind of lifestyle, he contracted AIDS."

"Jack, as if it weren't enough for people to persecute Foucault while he lived, you actually feel you must persecute him beyond the grave."

"What sort of persecution are you talking about?"

"Inventing knowledge, moral knowledge, in order to condemn him—that's persecution. He just didn't fit your mold, so you feel you have to appeal to 'morality' to make him fit it."

"Well, Carla, have you ever considered that perhaps the *world* has a mold? That the world is constructed in such a way that if you choose to do certain things, you cannot fit in the universe, and you therefore cannot prosper?"

"What do you mean?"

"You speak of Michel Foucault as a persecuted and wronged man. But the fact is that the greatest harm he experienced did not come from other human beings or their worldviews. He died because he engaged in acts that his body was not made to do. By living an immoral life, he thought he was exposing the sinister nature of others' thinking. In fact, he exposed the sinfulness of his own. Religion—Christianity in particular—did not kill Michel Foucault. Postmodernism did."

"Oh, Jack, at this point there are so many things I could say to refute what you've just said. But I'm going to leave this Foucault thing alone and instead focus on something that has not been discussed—something far more important. There's been a lot of talk about my view of knowledge being unworkable. But you all seem to have forgotten that what I have said about knowledge is based on what I said about foundationalism. *There is no foundation for knowledge.* History proves that pretty well, I think. Jack, you may not like where my worldview ends up, but you cannot deny where it starts."

"Carla, I have to admit that this really is one of the finest points that you develop. I think you have done an excellent job demonstrating that modernism's epistemological foundation has real problems. You have shown that reason cannot function as the foundation for knowledge. It takes *faith* to say that, and the history of Western philosophy demonstrates that this is a faith not everyone shares. Furthermore, if reason alone is the foundation, we are not able to verify some of the things that are most important to our existence. We have no explanation for the laws of logic, the laws of morality, and the uniformity of nature. These three things are things that modernism holds dear but cannot defend if reason informed by science is the foundation for all knowing.

"So, Carla, I agree with your observations regarding the problems in modernism. I disagree, however, with your conclusion. You say that modernism's foundation is indefensible, but then you conclude that there must not be a foundation for knowledge. *I cannot agree with this, because it is unlivable.* If you say there is no foundation for knowing, then you must conclude that we cannot know—that therefore logic, morality, and science are all uncertain, variable, and subjective. And the fact is that no one can live consistently with that view. Sooner or later we all have to face the fact that we cannot live without truth. In fact, trying to do so can kill a person—as it killed Foucault."

"OK, then what is your foundation for knowledge?" Carla asked in a critical voice.

> *The problem with postmodernism is that it is too much like modernism.*

"God—to state it simply. You see, the problem with postmodernism is that it is too much like modernism. Modernism started by pushing God to the side and placing reason at the center, as the foundation for knowledge. In time modernism couldn't find any place for God. Thus, it endeavored to live all of life without God. Postmodernism came along and said, 'Hey, if modernism is right about God, then it must be wrong about reason and knowledge.' Hence, it concluded that we must become willing to live without truth. My contention, however, is that postmodernism isn't radical enough. It needs to realize that modernism was *not* right about God. *We cannot live without truth, and we cannot have truth without God."*

"I'm not sure I can hold any more," I said as we three kids left the table for a seat at the snack bar. "My head's full of philosophy stuff. It's all smearing together, like when I pour too much gravy over my potatoes and it makes soup with the peas, and gets my bread soggy, and mixes—"

"Stop!" Brad snapped, looking disgusted. Normally a gross sort of guy, Brad gets a weak stomach when he eats. I love to make him sick.

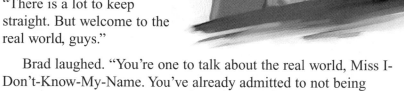

"I know what you mean," Guide Girl said. "There is a lot to keep straight. But welcome to the real world, guys."

Brad laughed. "You're one to talk about the real world, Miss I-Don't-Know-My-Name. You've already admitted to not being real, and you're talking to us about the real world?"

"Honestly, Brad, you must realize how complicated your world is. It takes some effort to learn anything of value."

"Excuse me for respirating. And just what do you think is the truth in my world? Can you guide us to anything more useful than a table full of talking heads?"

"Probably not. The table is likely to be the most helpful device I can show you, because the discussion there deals with the most important topic possible. Do you realize that any other worthy question you may have asked would have led to a similar discussion? All worthy questions hinge on ultimate questions, because how one answers ultimate questions determines one's worldview. That's what these people differ over: their worldviews. Call them religions or philosophies or whatever, worldviews determine how you think and act about everything.

"As for guiding you into truth, I point you to the people at the table. Even if you refuse to believe that any of them has the answer, they have at least showed you how to investigate the problem."

"Do you think any of them has the answer?" I asked her.

"Yes, I do. You have saved for last the one I think is right."

"Jack, huh? He's the Christian, right?"

"I'll let him tell you, Brad." Guide got up, ate her last cracker, and headed back to the table.

"I would love for all this to suddenly be clear," I told Brad.

"I have a feeling it won't be. Sometimes I think it will take a miracle for anyone to know the truth." We headed back to the table.

Jack looked at us for a long second after we sat down. Then that low, rich voice began.

"I am very happy to outline for you the history and tenets of the religion called Christianity. For the sake of this discussion, I do not intend to limit my description to any particular denomination or sect, just as my colleagues have attempted neutrality within the scope of beliefs they represent. I will begin with the testimony of history, if I may for the moment assume its relevance. Later I will show why Christianity allows history to be a credible witness." Jack smiled kindly at Carla, who raised her eyebrows.

"Christianity properly begins with God's creation of the universe and world. Christianity includes everyone who has ever been in a right relationship to the one true God, reaching back long before the term *Christian* existed. God chose one particular nation, called Israel, for the accomplishment of His purposes. Of course, many people outside that nation have been right with God, and many within Israel have not been right with Him. I shall explain the purpose of Israel toward the end of my presentation. For the tracing of history it is necessary to know only that Christianity is the continuation of a single faith that began with the dawn of humankind.

"At the birth of Jesus of Nazareth some two thousand years ago, the Christian era began. Exactly who Jesus was and why He was important I will also explain momentarily, but know that many people believed Him to be a figure prophesied in the holy writings of Israel. This figure bears the title *Messiah* in the language of Israel, a word meaning 'anointed' or 'designated.' Translated into Greek, the common language of the day, Messiah is *Christ.* Thus Jesus is called the Messiah, or the Christ. His followers came to be known as Christians.

"We know that Christianity spread from Palestine north to Armenia and Russia, east to India and China, and south to Africa. But we know relatively little about the history of those early movements. The spread of Christianity westward is well documented, for it was Europe that embraced it most. Christians grew increasingly numerous in the Roman Empire until the Emperor Constantine found it politically expedient to legalize Christianity in the year 313.

"Christianity eventually became the official religion of the empire, not long before the empire's dissolution at the hands of invading barbarians. Thus two great movements occurred in parallel: religious transformation by the spread of Christianity, and political disintegration

due to the fall of Rome. By the time the Roman Empire was gone, the church in Rome, which had enjoyed the most prestige, was gradually recognized as the preeminent church of Christianity. Gaining state sanction had mixed effects on the Christian church; on the positive side, Christianity spread to the masses of barbarians and sank deep roots into European culture that shaped all of subsequent western history. Those barbarians were, of course, the ancestors of the great majority of modern Europeans, North Americans, Latin Americans, and Australians. On the negative side, official recognition diluted Christianity's authenticity because everyone was required by law to be Christian.

"Though political control disintegrated into the feudal system, the church remained a unifying force and a preserver of knowledge and piety. During the Middle Ages, the eastern churches split off from Rome and formed what is now known as the Eastern Orthodox churches. Toward the end of the Middle Ages, two new movements coincided in Europe. In the political realm, nations formed, leading to a surge of intellectual and economic activity. In religion, groups of Christians broke away from the Roman church in what is known as the Protestant Reformation, which began in the early 1500s. Reacting against false doctrine, excesses, and abuses in the church hierarchy, the Reformers founded a number of new denominations.

The Christian church . . . is actually larger and more widespread than ever before.

"Largely through the reach of European imperialism, Christian missions spread all around the world in the following centuries. Imperialism is over, but the cultural influence of the West continues, much of which arises from Christianity. The Christian church may appear weaker than before—perhaps its political influence has indeed waned—but it is actually larger and more widespread than ever before."

"Wait, Jack; what is *imperialism?*" I asked.

"Imperialism is the political and economic dominance of one nation by another. From the eighteenth through the twentieth centuries, European countries established empires of colonies around the world. Imperialism had many bad effects on the subjugated lands, but some benefits as well. For example, the imperial colonies generally enjoyed more peace and prosperity than they had before. The greatest benefit, as I see it, was that the Christian gospel was able to spread more quickly and widely than it had before. Of course, one must agree that Christianity is good before he will agree with that.

"Now, if I may leave history and turn to the heart of the issue before us, I will summarize key Christian beliefs. As I said earlier, I intend to say what Christians purportedly believe. (*"Purportedly?"* I whispered to Guide Girl. "It means *supposedly,"* she whispered back.)

"First, let's discuss what Christians believe about the Bible. The Bible is composed of sixty-six books written by at least forty authors over fifteen hundred years. It contains many different types of literature and has sophisticated internal relations—each part must be understood in its place within the whole. It is not simply a guidebook or a list of dos and don'ts; it is God's revelation of Himself to man."

Brad asked his favorite question: "How do we know it introduces God? Who says so?"

"The Bible says so. At this point I do not wish to offer logical reasons to believe the Bible (though they are available), but simply to explain what the Bible claims and what Christians believe.

"The Bible also teaches that it is a collaboration of God with human authors. God worked through the human authors, in different ways at different times, to produce the Bible exactly as He wished it to be. Sometimes He spoke directly; often He steered the authors to write what He wanted without speaking directly. We get this picture from verses like II Peter 1:21: 'The prophecy came not in old time by the will of man: but holy men of God spake as they were moved by the Holy Ghost.' Christian theologians call this process *inspiration,* the English word used to translate a very specific Greek word used in II Timothy 3:16. It literally means 'breathed out by God.' The image is something like a musician playing a saxophone. Musician and saxophone are different things, but the two work together in one action. The musician supplies the guiding creative thought as well as the breath, while the saxophone is his instrument. However we picture it, inspiration is a supernatural synthesis of God's work with man's. It results in a document that can and should be called 'the Word of God.' "

"Is only the Bible inspired like that?" Guide Girl asked.

"Yes. We can trace the process by which the books of the Bible were recognized as such by the church, but ultimately the Bible's existence is a miracle. No human gave it authority or validity. It is what it is by the activity of God."

"Well, that's what *you* say," Brad corrected Jack.

"No, that's what the Bible says about itself," Jack corrected Brad's correction. "The verses I just quoted demonstrate that the books of the Bible were God's Word when each was written. What individuals, churches, and councils did afterwards was simply to *recognize* what God had done."

"But still, what you're saying is convincing only if you *assume* that the Bible is reliable," Brad corrected Jack's correction of Brad's correction of Jack. "You first have to prove that the Bible is a reliable book—something that we ought to trust, right?"

"That really is outside the parameters of what I'm trying to do in this presentation, Brad. I'm telling *what* Christians believe, not *why.* But since your question is very important, I will at least begin to answer it. Let me start by asking you a question. What sort of proof would convince you that the Bible ought to be trusted?"

"Well, I don't know. I mean, I guess a couple of things. The Bible should be logically consistent, obviously. And it ought to make some really impressive claims and then live up to them."

"What kind of claims?"

"Accurately telling the future would be pretty impressive."

"Well, Brad, you have just demonstrated that you are indeed a modernist. You see, your answer indicates that you take reason (with the help of science) as the foundation for knowing. Or, to change the analogy a little, you view reason/science as the 'machine' that makes the 'uncertain' the 'known.' When you encounter something that claims to be true but that you doubt, you want to stick it into the 'reason/science machine.' If it comes out of the machine with the stamp 'reasonable,' then you take it as true. If it doesn't, then you say it's not true—or that it at least cannot be called 'known.' "

"And this is the wrong view?"

"It's not the Christian view, that's certain," Jack replied.

"So reason and science aren't important to Christians?"

"Oh, no. I didn't say that. Sound reasoning and good evidence are very important in the Christian worldview. The Bible uses both repeatedly. In fact, the two criteria you mentioned for proving the Bible—logical consistency and predicting the future—are both found in Scripture from beginning to end."

"OK, so reason is important to Christians, but it's just not *really* important," Brad said with a confused look on his face.

"Reason is important to the Christian worldview, but it is not taken as the foundation for knowledge—as it is with the modernist's worldview."

"Then what is your foundation for knowing?"

" 'The fear of the Lord is the beginning of knowledge.' That's what Proverbs 1:7 says, which I take to be the thesis statement for the Book of Proverbs. This is a very important book in the Bible. It's a philosophy book of sorts. Through several lengthy discourses and through many short aphorisms (proverbs), it aims to prepare young people for productive, successful lives. Like any treatise on philosophy, some of it is speculative and some of it is very practical. Now, of course, fundamental to any serious discussion of philosophy are one's beliefs regarding epistemology. The Book of Proverbs is no different. It begins its treatment of philosophy and how it relates to success in life by talking about the basis for knowing something. But unlike many philosophical treatises, Proverbs boldly states that knowledge is not founded on experience or reason. *The foundation for all knowing is 'the fear of the Lord.' *"

"Jack, I'm afraid none of us know what this 'fear of the Lord' thing is," I added to the conversation.

"It means to fear God—but not just any God. Behind the English word 'Lord' is the Hebrew word *Jehovah*. This is the personal name for the God of the Bible. By 'the *fear* of the Lord' Proverbs means something like '*total devotion* to this God.' So what is being said here is that the foundation for knowing is nothing other than a right relationship with Jehovah. A human is able to 'know' only if he is totally devoted to the God of the Bible."

"Whoa! So you are the only person here who *knows* anything?" It didn't take Brad long to connect the dots.

If one does not fear the Lord . . . , then one cannot know something with certainty.

"Yes. But let me add that I do not doubt that you *think* you know many things. And since many of those things are things that I know to be true, I don't doubt that they are true. My point, however, is that without the fear of the Lord a person does not have a good reason for knowing what he thinks he knows. Certainly secular thinkers have come to a similar conclusion. Postmodernism states that 'knowing' cannot be justified—that knowledge should not be viewed as certain. If one does not fear the Lord (as late modernists and postmodernists do not), then one cannot know something with certainty. I think that the fundamental assertions of postmodernism are a secularist restatement of Proverbs 1:7. Our secular society does not fear the Lord, and our secular society is left without a 'beginning' for knowledge."

"OK, well, where is all this going? I think I've lost track of what we're supposed to be talking about." I really was lost.

"A few minutes ago I said that the Bible is God's Word, and Brad said that that was just my opinion. I told him that it was what the Bible taught. Then he countered that unless I could prove that the Bible was reliable, it was still little more than just my opinion. Then I demonstrated to him that he was trying to examine the Bible with an epistemological foundation that the Bible does not hold to."

"And why did you do this?"

"To demonstrate that you cannot prove the Bible's reliability unless you approach knowledge the way the Bible does—unless you agree that knowledge is possible only if you are rightly related to Jehovah. I could have given you and Brad an impressive list of reasons for believing the Bible is true, but I chose not to. For though these reasons are *impressive*, they are *convincing* only if you view the world the way the Bible says you must—only if you begin where it begins: 'The fear of the Lord is the beginning of knowledge.' "

"Well, this is certainly interesting," Brad concluded. "Go ahead and tell us more about your worldview and your ideas about knowledge."

Jack cleared his throat and continued. "A Christian's basis for believing in reliable knowledge is the Being and Person of God. In other words, because we believe in God, who created everything and knows everything, we believe that it is possible to learn and know truth. It is not difficult to believe that what I see or what someone tells me can be true, because the universe consists of knowable facts. What God knows to be true is what is true; therefore, it is possible for me to share God's knowledge and, as a result, know truth.

"At various times in history, God has demonstrated that He can communicate in any form He chooses. He may use dreams or visions, He may appear and speak directly, He may send an angel or a prophet, or He may inspire a divine book for us to read. I am not presently attempting to prove that the Bible is true, but only that if we posit the existence of an absolute God, the existence of a book revealing Him to man is perfectly acceptable.

"I said I would validate the use of history. Let me do so now. History books are not inspired revelation like the Bible. They are potentially fallible because human beings make errors and even tell lies—the Bible says so. However, if it is possible for human beings to know something that is true, then it is also possible for them to record and transmit truth. When history comes from multiple corroborating witnesses, it becomes *likely* that history is reliable, at least in part. Therefore, the Christian worldview allows for the use of history as a witness to truth, though never as the final authority on truth."

Jack paused and waited for questions, but we had none. He gathered his thoughts and continued. "Now that I have set before you what the Bible claims about itself, let me explain what it says about God and man. There is no elaborate treatise on God; instead, the Bible reveals what He is like through records of His words and actions. Christian theologians often summarize the Bible's portrait of God with lists of His characteristics, which they call attributes or perfections. God's perfections tend to fall into two general

EXAMPLES OF GOD'S PERFECTIONS	
Non-moral	Moral
All-powerful	Good
All-knowing	Merciful
Eternally existing	Wise
Never-changing	Patient
	Just
	Generous

categories, those that are independent of morality and those that are of a moral nature. The first category usually describes God's abilities: He is all-powerful, all-knowing, eternally existing, and never-changing. The second category contains endless superlative qualities, such as good, merciful, wise, patient, just, and generous. This great and good God is the Creator of all, the Preserver of all, and the governing Lord of all.

"God's relationship to man began with His creation of man. God created mankind as male and female, gave them the unspoiled earth as their home, and provided everything necessary for their happiness. They are commonly referred to by the names Adam and Eve. They were perfectly righteous. It was their inherent nature to be and do good. They were made in God's own image."

"Made in God's image? And that means . . . uh . . . what?" This was from me.

"The context of Genesis 1–2 indicates that the image of God in man is a group of characteristics that makes man different from the rest of God's creation. When we look at Scripture as a whole, and at the things that make us different from the other creatures, we learn that it is most likely that combination of intelligence, will, and emotions that enables one to interact with God. It does not mean that we are just like God. It does mean, however, that humans are like God in many ways—in enough ways that it is possible for them to enjoy a relationship with Him.

"However, God also made Adam and Eve in such a way that it was possible for them to disobey Him and so lose their righteous condition. Through the temptation of a third party, a being later identified simply as *Satan* ('the Enemy'), the first man and woman failed their test.

"In rebelling against God, they became rebellious by nature. It became instinctive for them to be and do evil. Not that they immediately began to do as much evil as they possibly could have, for the continued presence and activity of God counteracted the damage done by evil. But the natural bent toward sin passed to their offspring. God had designed living things to reproduce their own kinds. Consequently, righteous parents would have produced righteous children, but instead evil parents produced evil children.

This evil nature became manifest in the first human son, Cain, who murdered his brother Abel. The sinful nature has passed to all succeeding generations of humans."

Brad broke in. "Oh, that's just great! Christianity says that everyone suffers because one couple made a mistake. Supposedly, we are all bad because of something someone else did?"

"Not a mistake, Brad—a rebellion. Nothing compelled our first parents to sin, but they did. Had Adam and Eve chosen obedience, they would have passed a righteous nature to us all. It was their privilege, by God's design, to set the course of their race. But because of their sin, all of us are born sinners. We sin because it is natural for us to do so."

"Why didn't God just not make a way for them to sin?" I asked. "Then they would have passed on righteousness to us, right?" I thought that was a good question.

God . . . does not always explain Himself to His creatures.

"Ultimately, I cannot say why. God has His reasons for all He does, and He does not always explain Himself to His creatures. I can say, however, that it is wrong to suppose that God should have done differently. You see, to say that God failed Adam and Eve by making them as He did is to question the moral uprightness of God. And to question God's morality is to assume that there is an absolute moral standard outside of God. But in the Christian worldview there is only one absolute moral standard in the world, the character of Jehovah. Thus, to question God's goodness is, in essence, to question the foundation on which the Christian worldview is built.

When a person does that, he begins rejecting what the Bible claims as its epistemological foundation—*fearing Jehovah.* For a Christian to question Jehovah's goodness is like Ted saying that he cannot trust reason as a reliable path to truth. Once a person starts questioning God, he loses his reference point for knowing, and he is no longer capable of seeing the world as it is."

"So what's the answer?" Guide Girl asked eagerly. "How did God rescue man after his sin?" Obviously, Guide knew about Christianity already. This was her faith, I remembered.

Jack smiled at her. "God had to punish sin. Nothing evil can be in God's presence. Only perfect righteousness can live with God and love Him. If man were to be restored, man needed to re-gain his righteous nature. At the same time, every sin had to be punished, and even one sin condemns the sinner eternally."

"Bad situation," Brad sarcastically commented.

"Indeed it is," Jack replied smoothly. "So bad that only God is capable of solving it. His solution—the only solution—was to take human form upon Himself, thereby creating new perfect humanity, which He can give to human beings, raising them to the righteous status necessary to be in His presence eternally. At the same time, as a human He could take a human's punishment for sin. But being God, He could absorb the punishment for all human sin in one moment of time."

"Whoa! What was that again?" I was too tired to swallow that much brain food in one gulp.

"By becoming human as well as being God, God was able to overcome both obstacles to man's salvation; He took the punish-ment we deserve and earned the righteousness we need."

"The punishment was destruction, wasn't it?" I asked then. "How was God destroyed?"

"Yeah, tell them about the punishment," Ted sneered. He had been trying to stay quiet, but failed.

"The punishment for sin is not ceasing to exist. The punish-ment is eternal suffering in the lake of fire."

"Oooh, sounds painful," Brad responded lightly. "The Bible really says that?"

"But God saved us all, right?" I asked before Jack could answer Brad.

"God does not save all human beings, if that is what you mean," Jack told me. He wasn't excited or yelling. He was very sober, and spoke very slowly and clearly. "Just as Adam and Eve could not remain righteous against their wills, so no one can be saved from sin against his will. The only way to be saved is to trust Jesus Christ for your salvation."

"What does He have to do with it?" I asked.

"He has everything to do with it because He was God in human form. God's taking on of human nature required His being born as a human and living as a human. That was the chief purpose of the nation of Israel, by the way: to provide the matrix out of which God in human form might enter the human race. Jesus of Nazareth was that miraculous fusion of divine and human natures into one Person for the sake of our salvation."

Brad: "And what exactly do I have to do to be one of the saved people?"

Jack: "You have to trust Jesus Christ to save *you* on the basis of who He is and what He did. He is both perfect human and perfect God. He lived a perfect life, earning perfect human righteousness. He died undeservedly on the cross, bearing the punishment for sin. The price that would take us eternal suffering to pay, He paid in His one death, because He had the infinite capacity of God. He rose alive from the dead—that is called the

Resurrection—and so demonstrated that He can overcome death with life."

Me: "OK, what would I have to do to be a Christian?"

Jack: "I assume you are using the term *Christian* in a broad sense. As far as most people are concerned, anyone is Christian who claims to be, whether Protestant, Catholic, Orthodox, or another denomination. But if you mean, as Brad asked, what you must do to be *saved,* my answer is obviously the same—trust Jesus Christ."

"Sure, but how?" I was getting a little annoyed.

"You already know how to trust. You do it all the time. You trust a chair to bear you without breaking, a car to carry you without exploding, food to provide nourishment without poisoning you. Likewise, you must trust Jesus Christ to save you."

"And I'll be saved when I die?"

"Yes, but you will be saved *now,* too. For to be freed from sin and have the righteousness of Christ given to you is to transform what you are. Herein is the supernatural aspect of Christianity, which I cannot explain logically. Salvation takes mental assent, but it is far more than your decision. It is a spiritual rebirth. You will no longer be separated from God. You will know Him, as human beings were meant to know Him all along."

Central to the Christian worldview is the person and work of Jesus Christ—"in whom are hid all the treasures of wisdom and knowledge" (Col. 2:3).

God Is God

Memory Verses: Romans 11:33–36

For a change, the three of us stayed at the table while the others walked around. We were discussing Christianity. "I'm glad this is the last one," Brad said to me from the depths of his folded arms.

"Yeah, it's been a lot. New words, new ideas, all bumping together. I never realized how much some of these . . . uh . . . worldviews were at odds with each other. These people really argue!"

Guide Girl asked, "What did you think of Jack's presentation?"

"Great," Brad mumbled, head still down.

"Christianity fits together pretty well," I said. "But there are some things I want to ask. Some things just don't make sense to me, but I know the others will ask good questions. Tell me something, Guide: Do you think Christianity can answer every problem? I mean *every* problem. Like why there is war and poverty, why the rottenest people get away with whatever they want, and what we're supposed to do about it. Or even smaller problems, like figuring out what to do with our lives or who we're supposed to get married to."

Guide was thoughtful for several seconds. "I don't know that Christianity can provide an answer to all questions. Like Jack said, God doesn't always explain Himself.

135

> *I believe that even when Christianity doesn't have an answer, Christ Himself is the answer.*

Maybe Jack could tell you more. But I believe that even when Christianity doesn't have an answer, Christ Himself is the answer."

"How's that?"

Her forehead wrinkled. "If what the Bible says about Jesus Christ is true, then He is the answer to all questions. To use your examples, I cannot explain why there is war, but I know that Christ is King and that He will one day bring perfect peace and justice. He can cure poverty—even better, He can make a poor person rich in spiritual treasure and happier than many rich men. Someday He will judge everyone who ever lived, so I know that even when someone seems to have gotten away with evil, Christ will make it right."

"Promises, promises," Brad murmured, then raised his head. "Why should I listen to someone who isn't even real? Are there no real people who are Christians? Can somebody with real problems, in the real world, be a Christian?"

"Brad, I'm a composite of real people, remember? That doesn't mean I'm a fake; it means I represent several different real people, people who happen to be Christians. I'm like a fable. I may not correspond to one individual person, but I could be any one of many people; thousands of people, in fact. By the way, has it occurred to you that perhaps *you* aren't real? I mean—"

She had to stop because at that moment Ted sat down and said, "All right, let's wrap this thing up!" The others took their seats. It was time to start Jack's cross-examination.

I wanted them to ask questions in the same order they had aired their views, so Ravi led off. "Jack, dear fellow, let us begin by looking more closely at the Christian Bible. You seem to stake all of Christianity on it. But is it really unique, I wonder? And if it is not unique, what remains to Christianity? What then makes the Bible unique? You claim it was written by God, yet you conveniently acknowledge that it was also written by men. If men could write it, how is it specially God's book?

"Does its uniqueness lie in high moral content? No, I say, for your Bible is quite laden with immorality. It condones and even promotes behavior that is elsewhere condemned by it. However, I do not condemn the Bible's value on that basis, for I level the same charges so often directed at Hindu writings. I can accept that your Bible is complex, artistic, sublime, mysterious, and that those traits justify its content. My only charge is that the Bible is *not unique;* it contains nothing but what men wrote and lacks anything to set it above the holy writs of other faiths. In summary, my question is, Why is the Bible alone God's book?"

Jack addressed the group without hesitation. "The progressive writing of the Bible, by different real humans in real-life situations over many centuries, yet making a consistent and coherent whole, *is* the uniqueness of the Bible. It is a miraculous conjunction of human and divine, analogous to the union of deity and humanity in Jesus Christ.

"To show the parallel importance of a divine-human Book and a divine-human Savior, I ask two questions. First, do I wish to pray for mercy and deliverance to a God who is wholly other than I, or to one who knows by experience what it is like to be human? And second, do I want to read for wisdom and guidance for life in a book written by a distant God, or by a God who, in the very writing of His book, addressed genuine human beings through other human beings and gave real solutions to real problems? In both cases I want the latter, the divine-human Savior and the divine-human Book.

Come on, what do those humans know about being an insect?

"The question then reverts to Ravi's second challenge: the Bible's morality. To rephrase his question, Is the content of the Bible worthy of its claim? In the first place, the question assumes a moral foundation against which we may judge the Bible. This is obviously impossible, because the Bible claims to be the expression of God's mind, and God's mind *is* the source and standard of morality. We cannot assume another standard without rejecting the Bible's claim from the outset. On the other hand, Ravi charges that it is inconsistent; morals in some parts seem to be violated in others. I simply point out that the Bible accurately records many sins without approving of them. Just because a major Bible figure does a certain thing does not make it right in the eyes of God. On the contrary, many characters serve to illuminate God's patience. He saves sinners, not saints. It is true that the Bible describes and records evil, but God is never evil."

Any hopes I had held of finding Jack easy to follow were smashed beyond recognition. Brad had a question. "This sounds like just another way of saying two things at once. You had a problem with that when Ravi did it, but now you say that Christianity does the same thing."

Jack answered, "The difference is that Hinduism affirms everything at once: everything is part of an ultimate reality. That reality is everything that we call human and divine, male and female, good and evil, or whatever. The Bible is the product of both human and divine activity, but it is only one thing—a book. Likewise, Jesus is both fully human and fully God, but just one Person. Jesus is not equivalent to the Bible. You and I are not parts of Jesus. He is distinct from all other persons, just as we are distinct one from another."

"But Jesus is only part of God, right?"

"The Bible presents three Persons that are together the one God—God the Father, God the Son, and God the Holy Spirit. Frankly, I cannot understand a relationship of three distinct Persons in one God. The Bible makes it clear that there is only one God, that Christ is God, and that Christ is distinct from the Father and the Spirit. It's a mystery to us how those things can all be true, but to deny any one of them is to deny the Bible."

Well, what do you say to something like that? I decided to go back to a slightly different point. "Jack, I'd like to know if our only source for knowledge about the Christian God is the Bible."

"General revelation, through creation and conscience, also tells us about Jehovah. General revelation means the evidence of Himself that God has placed for all mankind to see. Creation refers to the universe in all its infinite detail, from the largest galaxies to the smallest subatomic particle. Creation is there, it is beautiful, and it is obviously designed by some guiding intelligence. Though it tells us nothing of God's moral character or of the way of salvation, it testifies to His existence.

"Conscience rests in every one of us, giving us the inner certainty that there is right and wrong, even if we struggle to define what they are. Why would there be any sense of guilt, of justice, or of retribution if we were mere animals? Conscience has no explanation without a higher moral reality.

"Yet conscience does not explain the way of salvation either. That falls to the Bible, which we call special revelation. Since it is intelligent communication of thought, it goes to individuals only as they give attention to it, whether in written or spoken form. Hence it is not general, but specific, or special."

I had a follow-up question. "So am I supposed to know God exists even without the Bible? That sounds just like what Ravi said about Hinduism: I should know it on the inside."

"Because we are sinners by nature, the general means of revelation never lead us to God by themselves. They demand special revelation, which is the Bible. The Bible illuminates what creation and conscience tried to tell me my whole life, but which I could not understand because my very heart was bent against it."

"But not everyone who reads the Bible becomes a Christian. What does it take to change that evil nature, as you call it?"

"A miracle. An act of God in which He makes a person into a new being by giving him life in Christ. We have no part in performing that miracle, but amazingly, there is something we can do to bring it about." He stopped.

"And that is . . . ?"

"Trust Jesus Christ."

I wasn't sure where to go from there, so I told Li to go ahead.

"Jack, I have a simpler question, one that to me makes Christianity's concept of God impossible. If God is both all-knowing and all-powerful, how do you explain the existence of suffering? If God knows about all suffering—even before it begins—and *can* prevent it, why doesn't He? It seems to me that the only explanation is that God wants people to suffer. But if you believe God is good and loving, that explanation won't do, will it?"

That's when Brad jumped in. The emotion in his voice showed that he was being more than academic. "That's right, Jack. How can you expect me to look at the suffering of the world and believe that God exists? Or if I believe He exists, that He isn't mean, and loves to watch us suffer our whole lives and then die?"

"So the problem of evil makes you doubt the Christian worldview? Well, Brad, let me ask you: have you ever considered that denying the Christian worldview leads to another problem—the problem of good?"

"Good is a problem?"

"It is if you deny God's existence. If there is no higher power or purpose, and if existence is bereft of any meaning, then 'evil' cannot logically be said to exist—so there is no 'problem of evil.'

But how then can you explain the presence of 'good' in the world? You speak of suffering, hatred, and injustice, but all of these ideas exist in your mind because you assume that there are such things as pleasure, love, and justice, and that these positive ideas ought to characterize the world. But where does that understanding come from if there is no absolute Being whose character defines the absolute standards of morality? You see, if you deny God's existence, *good* becomes an even greater problem than evil."

Since Ted had been third to present his worldview, he was third to grill Jack. "What I want to do is go back to the end of my presentation of humanism. Jack, you claimed that my worldview is faith based. Now let's suppose I concede that point (which of course I don't). Nevertheless, you still haven't demonstrated that your worldview is *better* than mine. We both have worldviews based on presuppositions—or so you say. Can you now convince me that your presuppositions are better than mine?"

"I cannot convince you to become a Christian—that is, to embrace my worldview. Only the supernatural working of the Spirit of God can do that. I can, however, demonstrate that only Christianity offers a consistent worldview. I can show that your presuppositions ultimately fail, whereas mine do not."

"I'm all expectation, Jack," Ted said smugly.

"Your key presupposition is that reason with science is the foundation for all knowing. Since you cannot find any compelling evidence for believing in God, you deny that He exists, or at least you deny that positing His existence is relevant to explaining and understanding our world. But I contend that the very entities you hold most dear in your worldview cannot be justified by your worldview. Without God, you cannot account for laws of logic, the uniformity of nature, or laws of morality. You say that reason and science are fundamental to knowing, but without God you cannot justify using reason and science in the knowing process."

"Oh, that's absurd. I don't need to posit the existence of God to justify my belief in logic and in the uniformity of nature. The idea of God is the result of wishful thinking. He's what you call an *immaterial* Being. In other words, a Being for which we have no evidence. We have abundant evidence for sound reasoning and nature, however."

"Are the laws of logic composed of matter?"

"Well, of course not. A law can't be material."

"Then how is it in a materialist's universe that—"

"Whoa!" Brad interrupted. "What's 'a materialist's universe'?"

"A materialist is someone who believes that only material entities (things composed of matter) are real," Jack answered. "And what I want to know is how is it in such a universe that one can justify the existence of logical laws. These are universal, invariant, and immaterial entities. They—"

"Whoa again!" Brad again. "Define 'universal' and 'invariant.' "

"Certainly. They apply universally—in all places, times, and situations. To be coherent, all persons must reason logically. These laws also are invariant: they do not change from person to person, or from group to group. So, Ted, how do you as a materialist justify your use of the laws of logic—things that are immaterial, universal, and invariant?"

"Well, I think that laws of logic exist by human consensus. Humans get together and examine the world and choose what they will consider to be reasonable. You don't need a God to have logic; you need only human consensus."

"Well, then you are a postmodernist. That's exactly what Carla was claiming. Each human community constructs its own understanding of logic. But, Ted, you scorned Carla for that view. It's absurd to suppose that logic and reason exist by human consensus. If that were so, meaningful discourse between two people from different communities would be impossible. We all sense that there is something universal and invariant about these immaterial entities. That sense explains why we're here arguing. We believe that we can have a meaningful discussion of worldviews around this table because we know that the laws of logic are not simply consensual. They're binding on us all—that is, after all, the reason we call them *laws* of logic."

"OK, Jack, then how do you justify your use of logic?"

"God. He is the absolute, universal, invariant, and immaterial Creator and Ruler of the universe. He made humans in His image and thus gave them the capacity to reason according to His own character. Logic is logical—reason is reasonable—because it reflects the thinking of the universal, invariant, and immaterial God. And that is how my worldview is able to justify these universal, invariant, and immaterial entities that your worldview cannot account for."

"Well, that's just nonsense as far as I'm concerned. I don't see how—"

"On what basis should we consider it nonsense? To say that something does not make sense is to assert that it is not logical. To assert that something is not logical is to assume that there are universal, invariant standards by which we are to judge things that claim to be reasonable. But your worldview is not able to justify such standards. So how can you say that my explanations don't make sense? I have a basis for claiming that someone's ideas do not make sense. You, however, do not."

"Jack, this is going nowhere. Let's change tracks. What about the uniformity of nature?"

"OK, do you believe in the uniformity of nature?"

"I do believe that the natural world is stable—that it will continue to be in the future what it has been in the past. Science would not be possible without such a belief."

"OK, what basis do you have in your worldview for saying that the future will be like the past?"

"From my practice of the scientific method. We've observed the uniformity of nature over many centuries of doing experiments. We conclude from science that this uniformity is part of the inherent nature of matter. The material world has certain properties that do not change. Therefore, we have every reason to expect that the future will be like the past."

"But, Ted, you're an evolutionist. You believe that our world is the result of a long chain of random changes in the natural order.

Fundamental to your explanation of the world's origin is the idea that in the past the future has *not* been like the past. On what basis then can you claim that in our day the future will be like the past?"

"Well, I would say that—"

"But even if you were not an evolutionist, you still could not account for the uniformity of nature. You say that past observations show that in the past there has been uniformity in the natural world; therefore, we should expect our future to be like our past. But this is begging the question. You're using probability to justify the uniformity of nature, but probability rests on the assumption that the future will be like the past. You see, you haven't justified the uniformity of nature. You're attempting to prove that the future will be like the past by assuming it. That's not good logic, Ted. And thus if reason is the foundation for knowing, your belief in the uniformity of nature cannot—according to your worldview—be considered something that you 'know.' You cannot justify it."

"And you can?"

"Certainly. In the Christian worldview, an absolute Being made the material world as a stable place. I can justify my belief in the uniformity of nature—and therefore my use of the scientific method—because I believe in and fear Jehovah, the God who created and upholds the universe by His all-powerful hand. You see, Ted, the irony is that you have to borrow from my worldview in order to use reason and the scientific method for the purpose of trying to prove that my worldview is wrong. My worldview can account for reason and the scientific method; yours cannot."

Ted just shook his head and then turned and looked away. Carla was the only one left. She looked impatient, I thought. I assumed she had something to do after the debate. "Jack, I've tried to see where you're coming from. I'm glad for all the contributions Christianity has made to world culture. I agree that the story of Jesus, with His gentle life, His execution at the hands of the establishment, and His Resurrection, is one of the most beautiful stories I know. But I believe we are examining Christianity, not Christ.

"My question is, very simply, what makes Christianity different from any other religion? Christianity became the very thing Jesus fought against and was victimized by—an entrenched religious hierarchy by which the elite held power over the people by inspiring both terror and hope. Will you try to persuade us that Christianity is better than the other views present around this table? Ted has to defend pogroms and concentration camps, but how do you explain the Inquisition? Ravi admits the problems of the caste system; do you admit the atrocities of the Crusades? Li can't explain how a soul can both not exist and continue indefinitely, but can you explain how a supposedly good and merciful God can condemn people to hell forever and ever, with no hope of ever getting out?

The thought of prisoners suffering in a World War II concentration camp may prompt people to ask, If God is good, why does He allow evil?

"And why does God supposedly do this—a worse atrocity than Hitler, Stalin, or Pol Pot ever dreamed of? Because of something called *sin?!* Just what is sin, anyway? You say God decides what sin is, but isn't it true that the clergy gets to say what it is that God says, either by interpreting the Bible or by getting messages from God? Furthermore, why is there evil in the first place? You say your God is all-powerful and entirely good. Since He's good, He should want the world to be a good place. Since He's all-powerful, He should be able to make it so. Yet there is evil. Why? I know you've already dealt with this in answering Li and Brad. But, to be frank, I found your answer less than satisfying. You've said that Ted's worldview fails because it cannot justify reason

How can your God send people to hell for being evil when, if He were really good and powerful, He would not have allowed the possibility of evil in the first place?

and science—the very things it holds most dear. Well, it seems to me that your worldview offers no good answer for the existence of evil. Does this make your worldview fall apart? How can your God send people to hell for being evil when, if He were really good and powerful, He would not have allowed the possibility of evil in the first place?"

Jack took a thoughtful moment. He didn't look disturbed. I guess he was used to Carla's venom by now. "Let me begin with your first concern. Carla, I certainly do not agree that our subject is Christianity instead of Christ. While Christianity may be a large and complicated thing, it has nothing of value to offer apart from Christ. Oh, it has much to contribute to every field of human endeavor, as you hinted, but all of it is bound to the Christ, the Redeemer of fallen man, the rightful Ruler of the world, and the embodiment of knowledge and wisdom.

"If no human being had ever followed Jesus Christ, He would still be the only way of salvation. If everyone who did follow Him continued to commit awful sins, He would still be utterly just and righteous. In short, Christ is independent of Christianity. The message of the Christian church is not an exaltation of its own righteousness but of the One who has mercy on helpless sinners. Conversely, even if Christianity had a spotlessly moral record to point to, without Christ it has nothing to offer to you, me, or anyone around this table.

"I could defend the church with examples of good things it has done, from its earliest times to the present day. But that leads only to endless bickering over the deeds of people long gone. I am much more concerned to focus attention on Christ and on God the Father.

"Speaking of whom, I will now address your charge, Carla, that God is guilty of a crime beyond any conceivable evil. You ask how a good God can send people to hell forever? Well, Carla, let me remind you that in your universe there is no problem of evil because there is no evil. You have no basis for criticizing the moral choices of my God because you deny that there is an absolute standard of morality. The deeds of Hitler, Stalin, and Pol Pot may have caused pain, but you cannot condemn them as evil, nor can you say that it is wrong for the Christian God to send people to hell. When you claim that my worldview fails to deal with the problem of evil (as Ted claimed as well), you admit the existence of something that your worldview cannot justify—laws of morality. And as I have already demonstrated, only the Christian worldview can justify such laws."

"Jack, you have not demonstrated that your worldview can justify moral laws."

"Yes, I have. In my worldview there is an absolute, good Being named Jehovah. His character defines right and wrong. Behaving according to His character is good, and living contrary to that character is evil."

"OK, well, I guess what I mean is that you have not shown why evil exists. How, in a universe ruled by an omnipotent and benevolent God, can there be evil?"

"Carla, to be honest, I don't know," Jack said, but without any fear or shame in his voice.

"You've got to be kidding! That makes your worldview no different from any of the others you've criticized around this table. This is perhaps the most important question for you to answer, and your worldview doesn't even address it?!"

"No, Carla, that's not true. The Bible does address the problem of evil. But it addresses the issue in a way that most people may find surprising. Consider the treatment of the problem of evil in the Book of Job. Nowhere in that book does God explain to Job why he is suffering—why he is being touched by evil. When Job questions God's goodness and wisdom, God reminds him that *He,* not Job, is the absolute and infinite ruler of the universe. For Job, the key lesson to learn was that when faced with the problem of evil, man must humble himself and trust God. The apostle Paul deals similarly with the problem of evil in his letter to the Romans. After anticipating that his readers will want to question God's goodness, he replies, 'Nay but, O man, who art thou that repliest against God? Shall the thing formed say to him that formed it, Why hast thou made me thus?' Carla, I'm convinced that there is an answer to the problem of evil. But whatever it is, God has chosen not to reveal it to His creatures."

"Sounds pretty cruel to me," she shot back.

"To those who have chosen not to fear Jehovah, I suppose it does. But leaving this problem unanswered does not amount to a problem for the Christian worldview. It rather substantiates its claims."

"And how in the world can it do that?"

"My worldview asserts that an absolute, divine Being created and rules the universe. It teaches that we are His creatures, made in His own image. When such a Being chooses to withhold an explanation from His creatures, His creatures ought not to question His goodness. As Paul said, it is not man's place to question God. We owe Him everything; He owes us nothing—and that includes an explanation for the problem of evil. You see, not having an answer for the problem of evil does not threaten my worldview, because my worldview posits a God who has all the answers but who does not need to share them all with me. In that vein, Carla (and all of you, really), let me ask you to consider carefully the following three questions.

"First, do we want a God who knows no wisdom beyond what we humans can understand? Or do we want a God who is so great and wise that He will, to some degree, do things that are beyond our understanding? Not that our longings determine what God is; far from it. God is immensely great and wise as a matter of fact. But I think that it is a happy and comforting thought, not a frightening one, that God knows more than we do.

"Second, do we want a universe in which evil—*any* evil—is tolerated? Once I came to understand evil as God does, to see it as a corruption of what He made to be absolutely holy and pure, then I too wanted evil completely eradicated. I want it gone from myself. I want to be purged of every last trace of evil, and I want to live in a universe free from evil forever. The existence of hell makes possible a universe that is free from evil.

"Third, who is responsible for our sins? We human beings are entirely at fault for our own sins. If God had not even made a way for us to be saved, He would have been entirely justified. He could have obliterated our race and started over, or just let us run our course until we destroyed ourselves, as we would have many times over if not for the continuing intervention of God to restrain evil. But God didn't end the human race. He chose instead to make a new race out of its midst. What is really hard to believe is that He saves any of us. Yet the truth is that He saves many of us—everyone who repents of sin and trusts Jesus Christ. His command to the entire human race, as it always has been, is to repent.

"In conclusion, I think you should consider that God has chosen Himself to be the major victim of the evil that results from sin. He sacrificed Himself to make our salvation possible. We are able to repent and be saved because of what He has done. God is thus doubly justified for punishing sinners in the eternal lake of fire; first, because we sin voluntarily apart from any compulsion; second, because we refuse God's gift of salvation, despite its being purchased by the sufferings of His own dear Son, Jesus Christ."

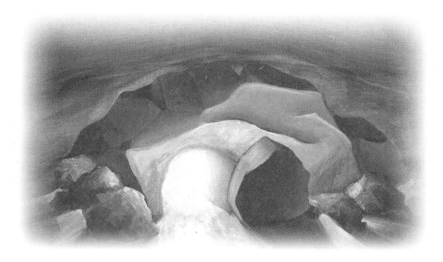

Conclusion

Jack was done. If there were to be any more questions, they had to come from us. Christianity was different somehow, though I couldn't quite figure out why. . . . Fortunately, Brad thought of a question. "So what does that mean for the people around this table? Are they all going to this eternal fire lake?"

"*I* would go to the lake of fire but for the sacrifice of Jesus Christ on my behalf. Nothing I have done has saved me from eternal punishment. Nothing makes me any better or worthier than any other human being. All that distinguishes me is the work of Christ, who will save everyone who repents of sin and trusts Him."

"Is that a *yes,* then? All these people, me too, will go to the fire lake unless we become Christians?"

"Unless you *trust Christ,* yes. That is what the Bible says."

Brad looked at me. "Clear enough? I'm done if you are."

"Yeah, I guess I am," I said.

"Great," Ted said as he got up. "Hope this has been helpful. Let—"

"Wait!" I said. "I do want one more thing. I want each of you to tell me, in a nutshell, what makes your worldview different from all of the others. Tell me how it is different as it concerns my original question about ultimate reality. You can go first, Ted."

"Sure," he replied, still standing. "Bottom line: I believe in what I can know. They all believe in things no one can know. How's that?" After I nodded, Ted walked away from the table and just sort of disappeared. I guess I shouldn't have been surprised.

I looked at Li next. He said, "Buddhism is the only one that gives true peace. None of the others really do away with suffering." He shrugged, rose, and was gone.

I looked at Carla. "All of them are ways a few people have tried to force their ideas upon and hold power over others. Mine is the only worldview that sets everyone free." With a toss of her head, she walked away and vanished. I noticed that the whole room was getting dark, though other people still moved in the background.

Only Jack and Ravi were left. Ravi arose with slow dignity, and with a smile delivered his final comment. "Only Hinduism fully satisfies the human soul, for only Hinduism realizes that man is one with the ultimate, absolute reality. All others either lessen or deny that glorious truth." He slowly walked away and faded into the growing darkness.

Finally Jack stood and smiled gently down at us. "In the Bible, God is God, and He is the Creator, Governor, and Finisher of all things. He is entirely free and independent. Glorifying Him is the purpose for human life. He has brought us salvation by His own power at His own expense. In all other worldviews, man is his own god: man is the measure of right and wrong, man is the agent of his own salvation, and man will ascend to deity." After a last long look, Jack turned and was gone.

The room was pretty dark now. The only light still on was the one right over our heads. Brad took the empty chair beside me and let out a deep breath. I pushed back from the table and looked at Guide Girl.

"What will it be?" she asked. "You've gone from being the Quester to being the Quaestor, you know." She said the two words just alike, but I remembered that they are different.

"Yeah. And the second one is a judge, right?"

"Well, in a manner of speaking, but not exactly. He really is a finance officer, like a treasurer or accountant."

"And that means he has to do what, exactly?" Brad asked.

"Do the work of a quaestor, of course. It's been charming getting to know you boys. I hope you enjoyed yourselves; I surely did. But I hope you remember that matters of worldview are not games. Worldviews are extremely serious business, and they determine how we live. Anyway, cheerio to both of you! I hope we meet again some day." With that, she rose and departed just like the others.

"So how do we get out of here, Mr. Quaestor? What do you do to wrap all this up?" Brad went on without waiting for my answer. "All this has shown me is that there is no difference between all these 'worldviews.' There's no way to decide which one is right. All of them are matters of opinion. I suppose that makes me most like Carla, even though I'd probably choose Buddhism if I wanted a religion."

"But, Brad, that proves they aren't all alike. Don't you see that you have to reject the others in order to accept any one of them? At best, Hinduism and Buddhism might be mixed, but you have to decide which of them is ultimately correct because they can't both be. That postmodernism stuff allows anyone to hold any worldview *unless* that worldview believes it alone is true for everybody and the others are wrong—in other words, all of them!"

"Yeah, that's it exactly: there is no way to know the truth. Do you have a way to tell me which worldview is right? Couldn't it be another one entirely, like Judaism or Islam or something no one has invented yet? Don't try to convince me you have it all figured out. I've had enough of this! I'm looking for the door." He got up and walked away into the darkness.

I don't know if I have ever felt more alone. All these ideas and no one left to share them with. I didn't have it all figured out, I knew that. But now what? *Like a treasurer or accountant,* Guide had said, *not really a judge.* In that case, let's count them up.

Hinduism: I am part of the one absolute being. Everything is illusion; there is no real good or evil. I will eventually be absorbed into the one being.

Buddhism: I am a karmic entity trying to escape the illusion of reality by realizing it is illusion. I will eventually enter nirvana, a state of bliss because it is nonexistence.

Humanism: I am an evolved animal working for the betterment of humankind. I will cease to exist when I die.

Postmodernism: I am a unique being, free and good, in a world full of other unique, free, and good beings. I don't know what will happen when I die.

Christianity: I am created by God, but I'm a sinner. I have to be saved by trusting Jesus Christ. If I do, I'll know God and be eternally happy after I die; if I don't, I'll be eternally miserable.

As I think back through them, one fact stands out to me. If any of the first four are true, what happens to me after death is going to be the same whether I believe them or not. They all have a general requirement that I be a good person and not hurt other people, but my future is pretty much set. Only with Christianity do I have to do something really, really different now, while I'm still alive. That doesn't mean Christianity is true, but it means I have got to know whether or not it's true. But how? How can I know? I have to be bigger than I am. I have to know more than I do . . . more than I possibly can!